FACE TIME

How the 2008 Presidential Race Reveals the Importance of Being **ON-EMOTION** In Politics, Business, and in Life

DAN HILL

Beaver's Pond Press
Adams Business & Professional

ISBN 10: 1-59298-259-X
ISBN 13: 978-159298-259-2

Library of Congress Catalog Number: 2008934665

Printed in the United States of America

First Printing: August 2008

12 11 10 09 08 5 4 3 2 1

Cover and interior design by James Monroe Design, LLC.

Beaver's Pond Press
Adams Business & Professional

Adam's Business & Professional
an imprint of Beaver's Pond Press, Inc.
7104 Ohms Lane, Suite 101
Edina, MN 55439–2129

(952) 829-8818

www.BeaversPondPress.com

to order, visit www.BookHouseFulfillment.com
or call 1-800-901-3480. Reseller discounts available.

CONTENTS

Part One:

INTRODUCTION

1 THE IMPORTANCE OF BEING ON-EMOTION

THE SAY/FEEL GAP

I can tell you the exact moment I decided to write this book and why. It was on reading a Gallup Poll, published July 16th, 2007, that reported that only 5% of Americans said they would not vote for a qualified African-American candidate.[1] Blame my cynicism. Blame my parents for taking me to see the German concentration camp of Dachau when I was six-years old. I don't care. Whatever the cause, I immediately, instinctively *disbelieved* Gallup's finding about the extent to which bias permeates society. I thought to myself: here we go again.

In 2004, only two of ten major polls were accurate in declaring the day before the election that George Bush would be re-elected. "Predictions burn pollsters, pundits—again" was the headline in *USA Today* two days after Election Day.[2]

No doubt, there are plenty of explanations to justify the call-out quote from the *USA Today* article. "Quality of information 'disgraceful'" one critic said. But my singular belief is that the problem of faulty research data rests in what I call the "say/feel gap," which is the tendency of people to spin, deflect, hint and hold back regarding their true response. The solution my company, Sensory Logic, Inc., has been using for a decade is a research tool known as facial coding. In simplest terms this tool involves scientifically reading people's facial muscle activity to learn how they really *feel* about something.

The "say/feel gap" will be familiar to you. For one thing, politicians have been known to tell a few lies. But there's more to the story than that. One of my favorite quotes is a popular one from West Virginia: "Everything in life is political, except for politics...which is personal."

In other words, life is hardly a rational enterprise. Intrigue dominates and feelings intrude. But in actuality, the opposite is true. *Feelings come first, as everybody* ***feels before they think.*** That's a neurological fact, as advances in *f*MRI brain scans have documented over the past 20 years. As we now know, people have three brains within one. There's our original, sensory brain, our emotional brain, and the relatively recent addition of our rational brain, where our verbal abilities reside.[3]

As a result, underlying the "say/feel gap" are two even more profound gaps: one between people's rational and emotional responses, and another gap between what is consciously known to us and what we subconsciously, intuitively sense and feel.

In short, a Gallup poll or any other kind of survey is fraught with problems. It can't readily access the quick, intuitive emotional response that drives people's decision-making process. In the business world, not getting around the "say/feel gap" hurts return on investment. In politics, however, failing to close the gap potentially has much more fatal ramifications.

Consider this quote from psychologist Drew Westen's *The Political Brain:* "Although the marketplace of ideas is a great place to shop for policies, the marketplace that matters most in American politics is the marketplace of emotions."[4]

The reality is that people vote their gut. Forget about complicated policy positions, which voters can't readily fathom and don't have the time for anyway. People vote their gut, meaning their intuitive emotional responses, which research has proven they reveal most reliably through their *facial expressions.*

FACIAL CODING: THE SCIENCE OF EXPRESSIONS

Lip service. Lying. Not knowing your own mind. Not admitting your true feelings to yourself. Not being very articulate. In essence, the things people *can't* or *won't* say. How to get around the say/feel gap is the issue. How can pollsters, companies and anyone interested in ascertaining genuine responses do better than a "*Casablanca* job?" By that I mean better than the famous moment in the movie when the jaded French police chief tells his men to "round up the usual suspects."

Here's how. The estimate from U.C.L.A. communications professor Albert Mahrabian is that in ambiguous situations (like asking about bias, or negotiating a business deal), 55% of communication comes through facial expressions, while 38% is through tone of voice. That leaves a mere 7% for the actual verbal exchange.[5]

Play the percentages. Ignore the words. Read people's facial expressions instead. But then you already know that because the expression *face time* refers to the benefit of having key conversations in person so that you can assess the non-verbal cues.

Facial coding involves, in essence, fine-tuning that practice. What is at present instinctive art can be perfected through the scientific method of facial coding. But to make you comfortable with it, let me explain how it works, starting with its three main principles.[6]

First, there's universality: even a person born blind exhibits the same expressions as everybody else. Think about that. This means that facial expressions aren't socialized. They're not learned. They're innate to all of us, a common biological legacy.

Second, humans have more facial muscles than any other species on the planet, creating a rich range of information.

Third, the face is the only place in the human body where the muscles attach directly to the skin. This means there's an instant, real-time, brain-to-face connection that controls all the muscles on the face. Spontaneity and sensitivity in the human face are the gifts of this system. Because nerve endings send signals to muscles attached directly to our skin, innate expressions are all but impossible to squelch. Attempts to manipulate others are thus more difficult.

Facial Coding: How It Is Performed

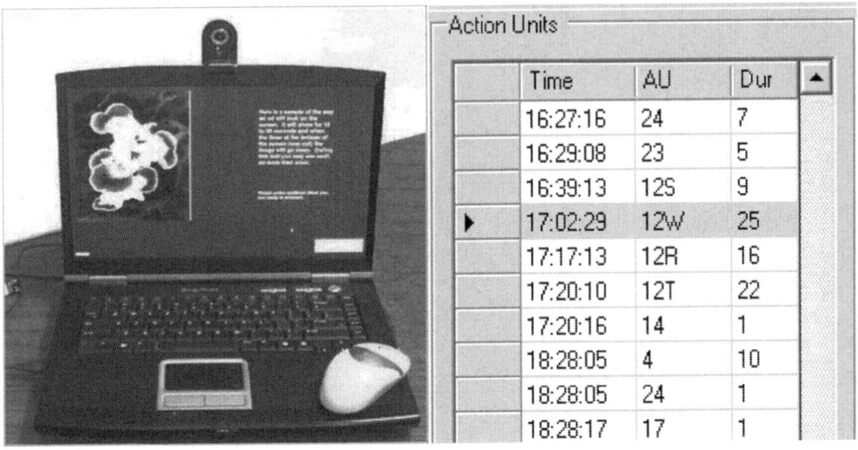

Action Units

	Time	AU	Dur
	16:27:16	24	7
	16:29:08	23	5
	16:39:13	12S	9
▶	17:02:29	12W	25
	17:17:13	12R	16
	17:20:10	12T	22
	17:20:16	14	1
	18:28:05	4	10
	18:28:05	24	1
	18:28:17	17	1

My company typically tests by showing people stimuli and questions on a laptop computer screen. As people watch a TV spot, for example, the web cam will record their expressions for later facial coding. At right, is a sample of what our raw scoring data looks like. We go second-by-second, even down to split-second intervals as necessary, listing which numbered facial muscle activity (or Action Unit) people are revealing. The timestamp facilitates double-checking the results. Each of the Action Units corresponds to one or more of the universal core emotions, and to our proprietary impact/appeal scoring system.

Charles Darwin was the first to detect this phenomenon. His observations launched facial coding. For nearly a century after he wrote *Facial Expressions in Man and Animals,* the tool of facial coding lay fallow. Not until the mid-1960s did psychologist Paul Ekman pick up the trail, refining Darwin's tool by creating his Facial Action Coding System (FACS).

Today, FACS is used by the CIA and the FBI for security reasons. As I confirmed from talking to a Halliburton analyst while in China on business, those agencies focus much of their attention on micro-expressions. Those are expressions people reveal on their face before they can suppress their innate reactions. A window into a person's true macro-level feelings may stay open for less than $1/10^{th}$ of a second.

I have been using the FACS tool around the world for the past decade, enabling my blue-chip corporate clients to measure and manage their emotional connection with consumers and employees. The advantage is that it provides a way to step over the "say/feel gap." As Daniel Goleman states in *Emotional Intelligence:* "Just as the mode of the rational mind is words, the mode of the emotions is non-verbal."[7]

In short, truly assessing emotional response requires going past words to the human body. Only then can the tracking become accurate. **People don't think their feelings; they *feel* their feelings**. Facial coding provides an opportunity to move beyond the rational and tap into the very fiber of the human decision-making process.

FACIAL CODING IN ACTION

In 2004, I first took my experience with facial coding into the world of politics. That year, I hit the campaign trail long enough to catch the Democratic candidates live in New Hampshire. I also coded George Bush and John Kerry during their televised debates. Coverage of my analysis appeared in *The New York Times*,[8] as well as on National Public Radio and on-line with Salon.com, among other media.

Now for the 2008 presidential race, I've applied facial coding more broadly, spurred by the Gallup poll. In fact, I couldn't resist putting facial coding up against its results to quantify the "say/feel gap." So to echo where I started, let's look again at what exactly Gallup did.

When the Gallup organization conducted its poll, their analysts asked potential voters: "If your party nominated a generally well-qualified person for president who happened to be (______________) would you vote for that person?" The **blank** was filled in five different ways. Voters were asked about **(a 72 year old)** John McCain, **(a thrice-married)** Rudy Giuliani, **(a Mormon)** Mitt Romney, **(a woman)** Hillary Clinton, and **(an African-American)** Barack Obama. Each voter was asked about all five of those profiles. But according to Gallup, the only type of candidate in trouble based on verbal admissions of bias was 72-year-old McCain. Here are Gallup's findings.

Besides the ridiculously low level of acknowledged racism, one other thing struck me about Gallup's results. That was the suggestion

Would you vote for a candidate who is ____________?	
Gallup Poll Results	**No**
72+ Years Old	42%
In Their Third Marriage	30%
A Mormon	24%
A Woman	11%
An African-American	5%

of an *intellectual alibi* in action. Now what I mean by alibi is that people will look for—and be relieved to find—a rational reason to support a gut-level emotional reaction. In this case, I suspect voters were most willing to admit bias against an older politician because the presidency is physically arduous. So admitting bias against McCain had a justifiable, rationalized excuse and could, thereby, be verbalized more easily.

A month after reading about Gallup's results, I had my company conduct some field testing of our own. With nearly 300 voters in four key states (Iowa, New Hampshire, Florida and California), we would ask about bias as well: "Would you be reluctant to vote for a candidate who is (has) (__________)?" Only in this case we added a second racial category, Hispanic, as a benchmark for gauging the African-American results.

During the testing, we recorded video of voters' faces during the one-on-one interviews. For each question about a type of candidate, voters were given 30 seconds to respond. Then we studied the video files, using facial coding to capture the emotions revealed during each answer.

Understanding the results is complicated by two issues. The first is that of the seven core emotions universally code-able using Ekman's FACS tool, only one—happiness—is a positive emotion. Surprise is neutral. The other five emotions we analyze with facial coding are all negative: anger, fear, sadness, disgust and contempt.

The second issue is that when scoring results, prudent market research requires a benchmark to understand the data. In the industry, this benchmark is called a "norm." Sensory Logic's norms reflect a decade of gauging, scoring and interpreting facially coded emotional data. In every study, we expect some negative feelings to emerge and, in recognition of FACS' negative tilt, set a high threshold for counting somebody as having a predominantly negative reaction to a stimulus or question. In this study, we set an *extra* high threshold. Thus we guarded against inaccurately labeling a voter as prejudiced based merely on uneasiness about having to answer six invasive questions in a row about possible bias.

Would you be reluctant to vote for a candidate who is (has) ___________?	
Sensory Logic Facial Coding Results	**Yes**
72 Years Old or Older	50%
Been Married 3 or More Times	68%
A Mormon	61%
A Woman	40%
An African-American	43%
Hispanic	47%

Here are our individual results compared to Gallup's: bias against a 72+ year-old candidate was up 8%; against a thrice-married candidate up 38%; against a Mormon candidate up 37%; against a female candidate up 29%; and against an African-American candidate up 42%. Meanwhile, prejudice against a Hispanic candidate landed within 5% of the prejudice expressed against an African-American running for office.

Our results suggest that Americans may not have come as far as hoped where prejudice is concerned. In short, the average amount of bias our test revealed was twice as high as what people verbally reported about themselves (51.5% versus 22.4%). The shockingly higher levels of prejudice we uncovered proved to be very close, however, to another survey on bias that I soon discovered.

In this case, *Newsweek* had asked not only how likely people were to vote for a qualified candidate who happened to be a female, African-American, Mormon or Hispanic.[9] They had also decided to ask the same voter how likely he or she thought their fellow Americans would be to vote for such a candidate. In the end, *Newsweek* found the same high level of self-reported acceptance of diverse candidates as Gallup did. But the *Newsweek* pollsters were on to something by seeing what voters would say when they also projected the question of bias onto their fellow citizens.

Do you think America is ready to elect _________?	
***Newsweek* Poll Results (Fellow Americans)**	**No/Maybe**
A Mormon President	65%
A Woman President	42%
An African-American President	41%
A Hispanic President	60%

By providing a deflection, a way for people to avoid acknowledging bias in themselves, the pollsters managed to secure more accurate information. In *Newsweek's* case, you can approximate the level of true bias by adding together the total number of fellow Americans described as either not ready ("no") or perhaps not ready ("maybe") to elect four different types of diverse candidates. On average, by combining "no" and "maybe" as reflective of prejudice, the level of bias is 52%—almost identical to my company's 51.5% level of recorded bias using facial coding.

The bottom line here is that the *Newsweek* deflection technique netted numbers that affirm our findings rather than Gallup's. So to get accurate, reliable results, **there is more value in reading people's faces than in taking their words at face value.**

Overall Average Voter Reluctance Levels		
Gallup	Sensory Logic	*Newsweek*
22.4%	51.5%	52%

ON-MESSAGE VERSUS ON-EMOTION

Talking points. Feeling points. Being rationally "on-message" vs. "on-emotion." Which is more important in connecting with people and winning them over? Brain science has proven the answer: people *feel* before they *think.* Emotion wins—and facial coding can play a key role in ascertaining people's true feelings, as I hope the bias data example has illustrated.

In the long run what's most important is that, thanks to facial coding, it's now possible to measure the "say/feel gap" and learn whether voters and consumers alike are really emotionally on-board. Moreover, it's also possible to give the concept of being *authentically on-emotion* the prominence it deserves.

There's a lot in that last statement. So let me slow down and explain its significance.

By on-emotion I mean two things: either personally feeling an emotion that fits the occasion or generating an emotional response in someone else that's appropriate to support one's goals. For instance, in politics getting your supporters all riled up and angry can be very advantageous. That's because anger is an emotion that's all about wanting to make progress or regain control of your life. Convince voters that the rival candidate, an incumbent, is blocking what they want to see happen and they'll flock to the voting booth to cast a ballot to remove that person from office.

In contrast, another way you can be on-emotion is to do what the legendary Democratic strategist and pollster Pat Caddell did prior to dropping out of political practice. Saddled with a client he considered a real loser, he decided to run the ultimate mud-slinging campaign. What was Caddell's goal? It was to make voters feel significantly sadder about the quality of politics. Then they would feel disappointed and resigned about the election's value—and choose not to vote.

It worked. Sadness is an emotion that slows you down and robs you of energy. So voters in that election responded to all the negativity by staying home in record numbers. They *felt* the strategy. And thanks to suppressed voter turnout, Caddell's client won.

Anger. Sadness. Disgust. They're all examples of feelings that drive behavior and outcomes. That's how human nature works. In politics, as in business or life in general, **being on-emotion is more important than being rationally on-message because emotions move people to action.**

A HUNGER FOR AUTHENTICITY

To this point I've addressed being on-emotion. But there's still unfinished business. I also want to share insights about the importance of *authenticity,* and its link to being *on-emotion.* Maximum value and opportunity are obtained when these two concepts are combined.

Authenticity will be on the presidential ballot this November, more so than ever before in American politics, given McCain's "Straight Talk Express" and Obama's "Change You Can Believe In." Why? In part, the answer lies in the country's recent political history. The ramifications of the Monica Lewinsky-Clinton affair and distrust about Bush's true motives for invading Iraq are still present in the American public. We have good reason to wonder about our leaders.

But the explanation goes deeper than allegations of public or private presidential impropriety. Today we live in a society of spin, of relentless corporate marketing, of permanent politicking, and the blending of the two forces of marketing and campaigning. Look back to the election year of 1968 and there's already evidence of the blending as it takes full shape. Writing about that year's election, Joe McGinnis opens *The Selling of the President* with a scene of Roger Ailes coaxing Richard Nixon to craft even a halfway decent political TV spot.[10]

In short, authenticity gains currency from contemporary commerce—a world of pervasive marketing—in which every*one* and every*thing* being sold to us is suspected of being a fraud. The new longing for authenticity reflects an indictment of commerce, of a world in which not only do individual politicians lie, but most corporate advertising promises are also seen as hype.

As a result, authenticity has, ironically enough, become big business. *Time* has anointed it as one of the top ten new business trends.[11] Tired of systematic artifice, consumers yearn for what's true. As business authors James Gilmore and Joseph Pine II observe in their latest book, *Authenticity*, the result is shopping based on "lightening-quick judgments of 'real' or 'fake.'"[12]

So all that said, here at last is where facial coding enters the picture, and how authenticity and being on-emotion link.

There are always two parties involved in any interaction, communication or transaction. There's the *sender* and the *receiver*, the candidate or company—and a targeted group of people being wooed. Facial coding works both ways. All of us are innately, instinctively capable of being facial coders. Even if you're not a real pro at it, while observing two candidates in a debate, for example, you intuitively judge whether they're honest and you base your judgement in large part on whether the candidates appear to be feeling what they say. In other words, even amateur facial coding enables you to evaluate two things. Initially, there's the question of whether the candidates' visible feelings are authentic. Next, there's the question of whether those feelings are on-emotion, meaning they're suitable for the context in which they appear.

That's facial coding applied to the *sender*. It's a matter of sensing whether the facial signals being sent are heartfelt or fake. But there's also facial coding as applied to *receivers*, referring in this case to voters. Now what they take in may or may not consciously register with them. Moreover, their response to it may or may not be truly acknowledged if asked about.

In its ability to get around those two barriers, facial coding has the power to glean new insights. To date, other bio-metric research tools like *f*MRI brain scans, EEG (scalp sensors) or EMG (biofeedback) can't reliably provide what facial coding can. **Facial coding alone can capture—non-invasively—people's real-time emotional response. Moreover, facial coding can report emotional response in more than just positive or negative terms**.

How valuable are these insights? In determining if someone or something is on-emotion, it's crucial, and actually may be everything. Remember the Caddell story? Both anger and sadness are negative emotions. But only one was on-emotion and key to making Caddell's strategy succeed.

In terms of the sender/receiver model, facial coding has a huge advantage over other bio-metric tools in evaluating a sender. It's not practical to slide a candidate into a fMRI machine during a speech, for instance. Nor are you going to attach sensors to candidates on stage for a televised debate.

Facial coding also enjoys an advantage in terms of evaluating receivers. That's because facial coding provides a scientific means of detecting and quantifying voters' responses twice over. First, facial coding allows studying live, real-time reactions to viewers watching candidates debate or seeing their commercials. Secondly, facial coding can also be used to gauge the way voters emote while verbally explaining their own views of the candidates.

As a result, it's possible through facial coding to report precisely a wealth of authentic on-emotion findings. You can start with the intensity and positive or negative nature of voters' responses. Specific emotions and their specific timing can also be measured. Finally, by studying all the results within the context of a campaign's positioning strategy, the vital question of whether the sender has been on-emotion by inspiring the preferred emotional outcome among receivers can be definitively answered.

There aren't any shortcuts here. For too long, the pundits and pollsters have relied on conscious, rationally-filtered dial testing that (supposedly) gets at people's real-time responses. But again: people don't think their feelings; they *feel* their feelings. So asking voters to move a dial one way or another, pro or con, in response to what they're seeing, is, as authors Gilmore and Pine might say, "authentically fake."

PRESIDENTIAL POLITICS AS SHOWCASE

The role of emotions, real or fake, has become an ever more central aspect of politics. You can track its rise from Bill Clinton's use of the phrase, "I feel your pain," during his 1992 campaign, to Hillary Clinton's misty eyes in that diner in Portsmouth during the New Hampshire primary fight in 2008. In an era hungry for authenticity and a more real emotional connection, candidates' expressed feelings have become a sign of their empathy as well as purity of motive and trustworthiness.

In 1972, Edmund Muskie appeared to tear up in response to *The Manchester Guardian* attacking his wife. But he chose to deny it, saying the moisture was from snow flakes caught in his eyelashes.[13] No longer is that the norm. In the wake of Michael Dukakis's failure to show indignation and empathy in response to a hypothetical debate question about his wife being raped, emotions aren't hidden in politics; they're showcased.

Feel nothing? Show nothing? From the sender angle, being more reserved or seen as an unsympathetic figure has helped to send the likes of Dukakis, Walter Mondale, and Bob Dole to their political graves.

The emotional displays of business leaders matter, too. I've written about that very topic in my previous book, *Emotionomics*,[14] and have facially coded famous CEOs for *USA Today*.[15] But unlike the typically closed-door world of business, presidential campaigns provide a dramatic, unique opportunity to study the sender/receiver emotional relationship. The 2008 race, in particular, has provided a great window into the emotional dynamics of building support.

Ways candidates try to connect

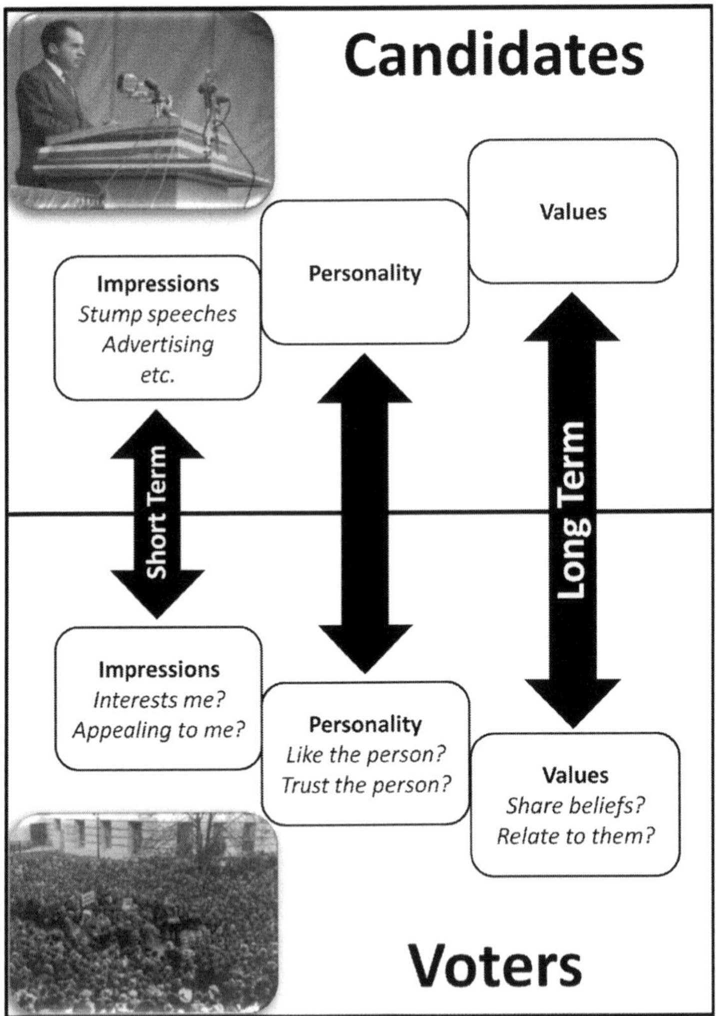

In the short term, voters react spontaneously to what they perceive about a candidate. Long term, however, voters' impressions of candidates turn into emotionally-based judgments about their personality and values.

For starters, 2008 is particularly notable because there's no incumbent president up for re-election or a sitting or former vice president in the race from either party. That hasn't happened since 1952. It's a wide open race, and the subsequent media attention has been unusually intense, leading to many more opportunities to scrutinize the candidates' ability to project authenticity and demonstrate their skills at being on-emotion.

Secondly, consider the diversity of this year's field of candidates. I decided to write this book, after all, on reviewing Gallup's dubious poll results. Call them tribal differences: matters of race, gender and religion. They're ancient and evoke emotional responses. The entry of Obama and Clinton and Romney in this year's race has heightened the emotional temperature, making it a good showcase for using facial coding to reveal emotional dimensions that might otherwise stay hidden.

Third, taking into account the on-going wars overseas, a faltering economy, and concerns about illegal immigration and healthcare, among other issues, this has been far from a humdrum election year. Emotions are running high, indeed.

Finally, for those of my readers who thrive on understanding case studies, a presidential election represents a Godsend. There are feedback metrics, after all: namely, election results. They tell you state by state, market by market, so to speak, how the candidates' strategies performed.

Speaking of business, I'm using the topics of leadership, branding, and communications to help frame an election story line that you already know and can readily follow. I'm doing so because nowadays marketing and campaigning are synonymous. **Then I'm adding the application of facial coding and the concept of being *on-emotion* to introduce new insights about how the race has unfolded to date.** What's the bottom line here? It's that to understand anything well, look for the answers on people's faces and you'll know what's in their hearts.

A FEW WORDS ABOUT STRUCTURE

From a sender perspective, the content of this book comes from my watching the candidates live and up-close in both Iowa and New Hampshire. For facial coding purposes, I've also watched all of their televised debate performances and numerous stump speeches on C-Span. From a receiver perspective, my company has in total tested nearly 400 voters in five states, using facial coding, to quantify their emotional response to TV spots and the occasional speech excerpt.

Altogether, including the study of the candidates' speeches and web sites as well as the reading of countless articles and books on the candidates, I've done my homework.

I could have organized the content chronologically or by party race for the primary season section. In the end, I chose to go with a series of vignettes that allow me to build Part Two of this book using a more thematic approach, based on leadership, branding, and communications. Then in Part Three I switch over to viewing the Obama versus McCain matchup based on quick top-ten checklists of those same three topics.

To the extent that it's humanly possible, I have tried to keep this book strictly non-partisan. Certainly, over time I came to prefer some candidates to others. But I always sought to give candidates from both political parties equal praise and criticism, as merited by performance and outcome. My criteria for evaluation was always meant to be the candidates' emotional intelligence, authenticity, and ability to be properly on-emotion as I have witnessed during the campaign or seen as a result of my company's facial coding results.

I can say that my facial coding training and marketing research experience gave me some advantages.

Therefore, I was able to predict correctly that Huckabee would emerge as more of a contender than anybody expected, and also that Clinton would revive her campaign in New Hampshire when the pundits and the pollsters were counting her out. Moreover, on New Year's Day evening 2008 in Des Moines, I told a Fox News analyst that, according to my instincts about the emotional dynamics of the Republican battle, Giuliani was already toast.

For most of my readers, I assume the candidates are generally well known. In text, I will refer to them only by their last name. The tricky case here is how to handle Hillary and Bill Clinton. Unless otherwise specifically noted by adding his first name, any reference to Clinton refers to Hillary. Here's a brief candidate overview to get things warmed up, and then it's on with the show.

Republicans

Sam Brownback, U.S. Senator from Kansas.

Dominant Emotion: Pride (smile with a hint of anger, lips pressed tight).

Fun Fact: Introduced the Broadcast Decency Enforcement Act after Janet Jackson's infamous Super Bowl Halftime Show "Nipple-slip."

Biggest Strength: Social Conservatism/Morality.

Biggest Weakness: A strange mix of tenderness and intolerance. A fusion of hellfire and Hallmark.

Rudolph (Rudy) Giuliani, former U.S. prosecutor and former mayor of New York City.

Dominant Emotion: Disgust (left upper-lip curls upwards).

Fun Fact: Officially became a Republican in 1980.

Biggest Strength: Safety & Security. Dropped crime rates in New York City and consistently pushes the war on terror.

Biggest Weakness: Combative, often bitter attitude (hence the disgust). Brings a prosecutor's mindset to politics.

Mike Huckabee, former Governor of Arkansas.

Dominant Emotion: Happiness, characterized by true and social smiles.

Fun Fact: Plays the bass guitar in the band "Capitol Offense."

Biggest Strength: Amiable personality. Huckabee comes off as fun, friendly, congenial and natural.

Biggest Weakness: Unable to build a brand-story. Pigeon-holed as the fundamentalist next door, without a serious campaign.

Duncan Hunter: retiring U.S. Congressman from southern California.

Dominant Emotion: Contempt (corner of mouth twists into a smirk).

Biggest Strength: Military defense, believes the military is a "unifying force in our country."

Biggest Weakness: Considered old-fashioned in both style and ideals.

John McCain, U.S. Senator from Arizona who spent over five years as a North Vietnam POW.

Dominant Emotion: exasperation (shown by his signature puffer-fish look).

Fun Fact: Wife is Chairman of the Board of the third-largest Anheuser-Busch distributor in the nation.

Biggest Strength: Honor and integrity. An unvarnished truth-teller who hopes voters value conviction.

Biggest Weakness: Fighter with a hot-temper, old and beat up (from the war).

Ron Paul, U.S. Congressman from Texas.

Dominant Emotion: Anger (often coupled with surprise, as if stunned by the state of affairs).

Fun Fact: Delivered more than 4,000 babies as a small-town doctor in Southeast Texas.

Biggest Strength: King of the internet; second most-popular candidate on YouTube (after Obama) and holds the record for single-day fundraising (mostly through online donations).

Biggest Weakness: Absolutist, generally unwilling to compromise his positions.

Mitt Romney, former governor of Massachusetts.

Dominant Emotion: Social smile (long, unnatural smiles).

Fun Fact: President and CEO of the 2002 Winter Olympics in Salt Lake City, UT.

Biggest Strength: Hyper-accomplished analytical type, with a legendary attention to detail.

Biggest Weakness: Tends to flip-flop on issues, most notably abortion.

Tom Tancredo, U.S. Congressman from Colorado.

Dominant Emotion: Anger, but emotes more rarely than most candidates, maybe because he's talking too fast to feel anything.

Fun Fact: Taught History at Drake Junior High in Denver, CO.

Biggest Strength: Conviction. Fervently opposed to immigration and even supports a bill to deport all undocumented workers (at an estimated cost of over $200 billion).

Biggest Weakness: Perhaps best known for his proposed solution to any future terror attacks by Islamic fundamentalists: bomb Mecca and Medina.

Fred Thompson: former U.S. Senator from Tennessee.

Dominant Emotion: Sadness and disgust (corners of the mouth droop while chin thrusts upwards).

Fun Fact: Spent five years playing district attorney Arthur Branch on NBC's Law & Order.

Biggest Strength: Comfortable, gentle image as the citizen-politician who is a down-home country boy.

Biggest Weakness: Checkered personal life as an infamous ladies' man who got his girlfriend pregnant in high school.

Democrats

Joe Biden, U.S. Senator from Delaware.

Dominant Emotion: Alternates these days between anger and a radiant smile.

Fun Fact: Began serving in the U.S. Senate in 1973, the sixth longest term in the Senate.

Biggest Strength: Foreign affairs, in general well respected for ideas on how to handle situations in the Middle East.

Biggest Weakness: Vanity, in love with his own voice.

Hillary Clinton, U.S. senator from New York and former First Lady.

Dominant Emotion: Broad social smile (long, fixed, and tight smile).

Fun Fact: After growing up in a conservative household, Clinton volunteered for the Barry Goldwater campaign in the 1964 Presidential Election.

Biggest Strength: Willpower, lifelong fighter who is perceived as both a nurturer and a warrior.

Biggest Weakness: Temper, perceived as a paradoxically hot-headed individual with an icy persona.

Chris Dodd, U.S. Senator from Connecticut.

Dominant Emotion: Anger, sometimes mixed with disgust.

Fun Fact: His famous dad, Thomas J. Dodd, prosecuted Nazi war criminals in the trials at Nuremberg.

Biggest Strength: Mediation and negotiation, his family nickname growing up was "The Peacemaker."

Biggest Weakness: Of late, the Countrywide Financial Loan scandal; he's received below market rates on two mortgages for being a friend of CEO Angelo R. Mozillo.

John Edwards, former U.S. Senator from North Carolina.

Dominant Emotion: Alternates between radiant social smiles and anger.

Fun Fact: As an attorney, Edwards won North Carolina's largest personal injury award of $25 million for Valerie Lakey, a five year-old who was nearly killed by a swimming pool drain.

Biggest Strength: A straight-shooting progressive, optimistic and outspoken.

Biggest Weakness: Seen as a hypocrite, fighting for the low-income Americans while living in a 28,000 square foot house.

Mike Gravel, former U.S. Senator from Alaska.

Dominant Emotion: Shows a mixture of anger and disgust.

Fun Fact: Moved to Alaska in 1956 and worked as a brakeman for the Alaska Railroad.

Biggest Strength: Conviction, fought fervently in the U.S. Senate to end the draft and to have the Pentagon Papers put into public record.

Biggest Weakness: Maverick attitude, not seen as reliable.

Dennis Kucinich, U.S. Representative from Ohio and former Mayor of Cleveland.

Dominant Emotion: Besides anger, given to disgust and sadness.

Fun Fact: Was elected to Cleveland City Council at the age of 23.

Biggest Strength: Confidence, always outspoken and adamant despite his diminutive size (5'6").

Biggest Weakness: Despite being seen as "scrappy" he is also described as abrasive, temperamental and chaotic.

Barack Obama, U.S. Senator from Illinois.

Dominant Emotion: Broad true smiles.

Fun Fact: From ages 6—12, he lived in Jakarta, Indonesia before returning to Hawaii until college.

Biggest Strength: Inspiring hope for change; seen as the possible catalyst to move the nation in a new direction.

Biggest Weakness: Lack of experience, only national political experience has been his previous four years in the U.S. Senate.

Bill Richardson, former governor of the state of New Mexico.

Dominant Emotion: Miserable smile, a grin-and-bare-it look.

Fun Fact: Raised in Mexico City by a Spanish mother and American father, until he moved to Connecticut at age 13.

Biggest Strength: Foreign relations, served as ambassador to the U.N. and also negotiated release of imprisoned aerospace workers in Iraq.

Biggest Weakness: Even among the country's Hispanic voters, not able to generate much excitement.

Part Two:

THE NOMINATION BATTLES

2 LEADERSHIP

Candidate as Product

OVERVIEW

Among the Republicans who ran for president in 2008, both McCain and Huckabee have written books about the importance of character in a leadership role. In McCain's case, it's entitled *Character Is Destiny*.[1] Meanwhile, Huckabee likes the concept so much he's used it twice, once for *Character Makes a Difference* and again for *Character Is the Issue*.[2,3] In comparison, conspicuously absent are any extended writings by the party's long-time frontrunner, Giuliani, on the subject.

As shown by our facial coding data, perhaps that's because of the big emotional bias against a leader who's been divorced three times. Or it could be because of how Giuliani's marriages have gone. His first one was annulled, after all, on the grounds that he had unwittingly married his second cousin, thinking she was his third cousin. The second time, Giuliani informed the mother of his two children that he was divorcing her via a news conference.

Whatever the explanation, Giuliani decided to stress his electability rather than character. But character does matter. For instance, business leadership surveys repeatedly indicate that attributes like being **trustworthy**, **inspiring**, **forward-looking**, and **cooperative** are considered highly desirable.[4] What are the other top-ten attributes of being an emotionally savvy leader? As I will soon discuss, they include: being **confident**, **stable**, **unselfish**, **positive**, **accessible**, and **energetic**. (For a full description of each attribute, see Appendix A.)

Soon I'll show how stories from the campaign trail illuminate each of those attributes. But first let's set the stage by showing how the Republican and Democratic contenders came across in debates, as an early indication of their leadership ability to be on-emotion.

RESULTS FROM FACIALLY CODING DEBATES

Here's a little context for starters. To do our facial coding of the candidates, my company chose four separate Democratic and Republican debates held during the late summer and fall of 2007. Then we analyzed each candidate's on-screen performance. The ground rules were that we coded any expressions shown by the candidates while answering a question, as well as any other time the camera zoomed in on them for a response shot as either a rival or the moderator was discussing that candidate.

As described more fully in Appendix D, our facial coding analysis involves seven core emotions that translate, in turn, into ten emotional states. We take the one true positive, happiness, and subdivide into four degrees of happiness based on whether a true smile, robust social smile, weak social smile or a micro-smile is shown.

In this case, surprise, often catalogued by us as a weak positive emotional state because of the desire of companies to create a "wow," is being treated as the neutral emotion it actually is. That's because debates are often, in part, about trying to "catch" candidates by surprise. So why not indicate how often they were either actually surprised, or else they feigned surprise for dramatic effect? As you can see from these results, Gravel and Giuliani in particular gave off signs of surprise, but they were very different. Gravel's surprised looks came and went naturally, as if he were genuinely amazed by the state of America. Meanwhile, Giuliani held his expressions longer, suggesting that they were willfully contrived, even theatrical in nature.

The five negative emotional states consist of frustration (anger), anxiety (fear), dislike (disgust and contempt), sadness, and skepticism. The latter refers to instances in which a candidate makes a negative or sarcastic comment while flashing a social smile to soften the effect.

The comparative charts shown below have been simplified into only three categories. In my commentary, however, I may allude at time to results from all ten emotional states. For instance, among the major, viable Democratic contenders, Clinton had the most smiles on stage during these debates. But her smiles were most often of the self-conscious social variety. As for the negative emotions, Hunter was the king of dislike, while Thompson led in sadness, Richardson in anxiety, and Romney in frustration (his rivals often picked on him in the debates).

What's the key finding from facially coding the debates? It's this: the Democratic field was much more positive. On average, 45.2% of their facial expressions were variations of happiness (smiling). In contrast, only 22% of the expressions shown by the GOP candidates were upbeat. Ronald Reagan was famous for projecting optimism. But no matter how much this crop of Republican contenders invoked his name, they certainly weren't exhibiting his trademark emotional outlook.

Four Democratic Debates: Emotions Shown

Candidate	Positive	Neutral	Negative
Democratic Avg.	34%	22%	44%
Dennis Kucinich	69%	8%	23%
Hillary Clinton	62%	23%	15%
John Edwards	50%	21%	29%
Christopher Dodd	38%	0%	63%
Bill Richardson	33%	17%	50%
Barack Obama	30%	30%	40%
Joe Biden	18%	18%	64%
Mike Gravel	9%	45%	45%

Grateful for the free media attention, Kucinich was the most upbeat; Biden and Dodd were the grumpiest.

Four Republican Debates: Emotions Shown

Candidate	Positive	Neutral	Negative
Republican Avg.	18%	15%	66%
Ron Paul	44%	11%	44%
Rudy Giuliani	33%	40%	27%
Mitt Romney	23%	8%	69%
John McCain	15%	8%	77%
Mike Huckabee	14%	14%	71%
Tom Tancredo	14%	14%	71%
Fred Thompson	0%	25%	75%
Sam Brownback	0%	0%	100%
Duncan Hunter	0%	0%	100%

Despite a great true smile, Huckabee rarely exhibited it as he treated each topic with concern. Only Paul and Giuliani enjoyed themselves on stage.

Now, let's see how the previously mentioned top ten attributes in leadership were demonstrated—or not—on the campaign trail.

CONFIDENCE: THE RESTORATION

Throughout the second half of 2007, Giuliani and Clinton each maintained their respective leads in the national polls. But as their political fortunes became shakier, only one adapted by jettisoning a characteristic facial expression that signals confidence. That person was Clinton. But since hers is a more complex story, let's tackle Giuliani first.

After the former New York City mayor lost in his fallback, firewall state of Florida, and dropped out of the 2008 race, the post-mortem analysis and confessions began in earnest. I found two favorite tidbits to dwell on.[5] Together, they exemplify the leadership sin of *hubris*—and the fine line that exists between exhibiting on-emotion confidence or suffering from the emotional indulgence of arrogance.

The first came from a senior policy advisor to Giuliani, who had told *The New York Observer* three months earlier: "I don't believe this can be taken from us." (How wrong can you be?) The second came from Republican consultant Nelson Warfield, who added: "Rudy didn't even care enough about conservatives to lie to us."

Truth be told, in politics, as in business, it's always a good thing to be sensitive to one's environment and sense when changes need to be made—before it's too late. Giuliani didn't, and so he suffered the consequences.

What stayed constant in the man was a "my-way-or-the-highway" type attitude, as attested to by a Bush administration staffer who said of Giuliani: "Either you love him or he hates you." The physical equivalent of that attitude is Giuliani's upper lip curl. To find it, watch any extended YouTube video and look closely at the left side of Giuliani's mouth. Sooner than later, you'll see *The Curl*. As facial coders and students of emotions in general know, it betrays his disgust: a visceral rejection of objects, people, even ideas, on the grounds that they "stink" or "taste bad."

The Giuliani Curl

I first saw The Curl in person at that rarest of events, a Giuliani campaign stop in Iowa. There, at a fire station in a west-side neighborhood of Des Moines, the mayor nodded and signed autographs at an informal gathering.

The whole, brief affair struck me as inadvertently comical. "How are you?" Giuliani would say to some adoring kid whose parents had brought the boy or girl along. The mayor would mean to offer a warm, welcoming smile. However, it barely registered either in his voice or on his face. (Maybe Giuliani was just in bad form that day.) But the lip curl was fully in evidence, putting a chill into that August day.

In Clinton's case, she was at once both the former and future queen, her husband, Bill, the king. Obama and Edwards and the rest of the contenders were either brave knights or knaves, depending on your view of them and their seemingly long odds of dethroning her. The Restoration was what she had in mind. ("Down with the monarchy!" yelled a heckler at one of her later campaign events.) Think of her campaign as a promised brand extension, following Bill; or a solution to the constitutional amendment barring a president from a third term; or perhaps instead a plebiscite on Bill's legacy of "peace and prosperity."

It doesn't matter. More immediately evident for everyone to see was *The Smirk*: Clinton's version of Giuliani's Curl. Yes, that expression signals assurance. It's the physical equivalent of the comment, "I'm no dummy," which I often heard Clinton say during her long stay on the campaign trail.

But The Smirk is, in fact, not so smart from a leadership point of view. That's because a smirk is a sure-fire sign of contempt, and contempt is an emotion that puts people off. Put another way, contempt is a stain. As an emotion, it shows you consider yourself (morally) superior to the other party you're addressing. And so it fatally stains the emotional tapestry of any relationship, whether professional or personal in nature.

Evidence of that fact comes from Malcolm Gladwell's best-seller, *Blink: The Power of Thinking Without Thinking.*[6] In it, he notes that the famous psychologist and marriage counselor John Gottmann has studied contempt expressions carefully. In running his Love Lab at the University of Washington, Gottman uses facial coding, whereby capturing an hour of video enables him to be 95% accurate as to whether the couple will manage to remain married 15 years later. Cut it down to 15 minutes of facially-coded video, Gottman's success rate is still around 90%.

Based on Love Lab results, what's the surest barometer that a marriage will fail? Expressions of contempt. After all, whether in working things through in a marriage or on the job, when you consider—and reveal—that the other party is not on par with you, it's hard to reconcile.

The sign of contempt is that the skin beyond one lip corner pulls inwards toward that corner. (Contempt is a uni-lateral expression, more likely to be evident in most people on the left side of the face, which is most people's more expressive side.) When that happens, the corner of the mouth also tightens and the lip corner narrows. I think of it as a little mouth-pocket tornado, a slightly angled muscle tension, complete with wrinkles or a bulge at the lip corner.

I suggest you think of the cartoon character, Snidely Whiplash, who by name and look was the embodiment of contempt.

Meanwhile, in politics, you need look no farther for Clinton's prominent fellow smirkers than people like George Bush '43, Dick Cheney, or Donald Rumsfeld. There's also Joseph Lieberman, whose contempt expression is so constant that during the 2000 race I used to joke that it looked surgically implanted.

Bridging the Partisan Gap: Fellow Smirkers

Clinton, Bush, Rumsfeld and Cheney: nobody shown doubts their abilities.

Once she lost in Iowa, Clinton stopped smirking. Not entirely, mind you, but relative to her previous level. Even for such a disciplined campaigner as Clinton, abandoning The Smirk could not have been an entirely conscious choice. No doubt, she felt less confident; perhaps she also recognized that it was politically detrimental to her chances for capturing the White House. What disconnects you emotionally from your spouse surely can't help with attracting voters' support, either.

Indeed, in the Democratic race post-Iowa, the Smirk all but disappeared. The one time I most notably saw contempt being expressed again was during Obama's primary season victory speech. Minutes earlier in her own speech, Clinton had pointedly refused to concede. Was it a stance that rattled Obama, got under his skin, as Clinton had so often done during the struggle?

Consider the moment when Obama climatically said, "I am the Democratic candidate for President of the United States of America." The first thing I noticed was the absence of a victory glow about him. Simultaneously, I noticed that it was as if there had been an emotional blood transfusion between him and Clinton. After making that statement, Obama paused, and then for the first time that I had seen him do so in nearly a year of facially coding him, here's how Obama emoted. Why, he *smirked*, briefly, and only once. But he smirked, perhaps thinking to himself that he could now play Clark Gable's Rhett Butler and say to Clinton, as Scarlett O'Hara, *frankly, my dear, I don't give a damn* (about you and your campaign any longer).

Let's grant Obama that as a momentary indulgence. The larger point I'm driving to here remains valid: confidence is good, arrogance is bad. Leaders need to understand where people are coming from. **Like another negative emotion, namely *fear*, contempt is an emotion that cuts you off from others**.

People who recognize that you're condescending to them will give up and won't make the necessary effort. They'll conclude that they can't please you. Great leaders have to be in touch with the emotional pulse of those around them. Be down-to-earth, heartfelt and aligned with the current climate.

COOPERATIVE: RIDING THE WAVE

What's the opposite of confidence that fatally turns into arrogant contempt? It's being cooperative, fair-minded, and inviting people into the process so that you, as a leader, can surround yourself with truly committed talent. In contrast, Clinton surrounded herself with advisors, a bunch of inside-the-Beltway consultants (on whom her campaign spent millions of dollars). Meanwhile, other candidates—by necessity or design—looked elsewhere for assistance.

One of them was Huckabee, so cash-starved I overheard him jokingly tell a fan at the Ames Straw Poll: "I can't buy you, I can't even [afford to] rent you." Unlike Romney's supporters, I noticed that Huckabee's were on-emotion, displaying lots of enthusiastic smiles on their faces.

Buttons were being sold that proclaimed, "I like Mike." Indeed, that was true. Emotions are contagious, and I could see that the affection linking this affable candidate with people around him would ultimately help Huckabee go much farther in the race than the pundits, cash flow, or the original polls would have ever suggested.

I shared my observation in a speech at the National Press Club in mid-September 2007. There, I ventured that Huckabee was "almost a natural vice presidential choice." My reasoning? That Huckabee's sunny disposition and conservative credentials could benefit either McCain or Giuliani.

Both *Campaign Insider* and *American Observer* quoted my observation in print.[7] In doing so, they attested to my faith in Huckabee's appeal three months before the *USA Today*/Gallup tracking data would lift him into second place nationally—far above the less than 5% support he had when I made my declaration.[8]

Parallel to Huckabee, Obama has also exhibited the ability to be affable and nurture the kind of collaborative support most leaders only dream of. What the two men have most obviously in common is the way they smile. The muscle around each eye relaxes, bringing a twinkle to their eyes. Among all candidates, they had the best, most relaxed, most vibrant true smiles when they exhibited them, which was rarely on stage during televised debates.

The Race's Two True-Smilers

Huckabee and Obama enjoying the public spotlight.

In the end, Obama would ride a wave of enthusiasm that dwarfed even the Hawaiian waves he saw as a boy growing up near Waikiki Beach in Honolulu. The numbers are staggering. During the primary season, Obama would draw crowds as large as 75,000, raise money from a donor base of over 1.5 million people, and get 4.5 million-plus viewers to take in his most viral video. It wasn't by chance. "Our belief was that personal contact was the important thing," campaign manager David Plouffe has affirmed.[9]

To that end, supporter-generated co-creation was encouraged. Obama supporters who went to his web site could develop their own blogs, send in policy recommendations, set up their own mini fundraising site, organize an event, and retrieve call lists and scripts to telecanvass at home.

Using emotional intelligence to foster a cohesive, cooperative culture is smart in every case. In contrast, the instinct of entities like big business is to go big and top-down. Clinton did it, too, with a slew of big-name endorsements, contributors, consultants, and the like. Meanwhile, Obama went small and very collaborative, bottom-up, and in the process obviously hit the big-time.

He also beat big odds. The morning after Obama clinched the nomination, I went to wait for my appearance in the green room at the Fox studio in Manhattan. There I met Karl Rove, Bush's brain trust. I asked him if he had expected Obama to win. Originally, I had him at "20 to one odds," Rove admitted.

On-emotion leadership is the key to success because success depends on getting people emotionally on board. What is loyalty, after all, if not a *feeling*? A leader who's broad-minded promises acceptance. That trait also creates ease, because people don't have to worry about suffering disgusted, contemptuous rejection. Huckabee's unexpected support and Obama's array of web-site clicks, donations and votes demonstrate the advantage of being on-emotion: **great leaders identify formal and informal points of contact and make people feel invited to participate and collaborate**.

UNSELFISH: "YES, WE CAN" VS. WILLFUL DREAMS

Integral to fostering a cooperative spirit is demonstrating a lack of selfishness. It's a vital link, but somehow it wasn't until the evening of the Ohio and Texas primary results that I finally, profoundly noticed the chants used by the two remaining, rival Democratic camps. The Obama supporters were once again chanting "Yes, We Can." By then I had come to understand it as Obama's brand promise, even his value proposition as a leader. The "yes" and "can" were both affirmative—a doctrine of *hope*. And the "we" was inclusive, signaling a co-creation role for his supporters.

In comparison, the Clinton supporters were chanting "Yes, she will." What was the difference? Their chant was, first of all, an echo of his. Moreover, their chant was mostly about her, her character, her legendary resiliency and willpower (in enduring the travails of her husband's serial infidelities, most of all). Her promise was singular, and then only through its pronoun also a nod to her path-breaking role as the first viable female candidate for the White House.

Her chant was affirmative, too, of course, an implicit promise that Clinton's fortitude would make a difference for the better in the lives of her supporters. But of the two chants, it certainly failed to rise above self-interest as readily as Obama's.

Were there worse instances of solipsism on the campaign trail? Yes, think of Bill Clinton giving a speech in Iowa. There a reporter counted Bill's use of "I" 94 times in 10 minutes (while mentioning Hillary just seven times).[10] Another instance I witnessed was at the Ames Straw Poll. There Brownback closed his speech by saying, "I have a dream." The dream: "that the son of a Kansas farmer can grow up to become the next president of the United States of America."

Now that may not sound so bad. What's wrong with dreaming, you might say. Every politician is ambitious. But for starters, the scale of the setting and occasion was all wrong. With his wording, Brownback was inviting a comparison to Martin Luther King, Jr.'s famous 1965 "I have a dream" civil rights speech delivered on the mall in Washington, D.C. This new speech was hardly so momentous.

Moreover, King was a great orator (Brownback is not)—and his dream was on behalf of an entire race of people. King's dream was set against the mighty historical background of racism and of seeking fully to secure and protect the rights of African-Americans as both fellow citizens and, indeed, respected human beings. Brownback's dream was, in contrast, nakedly about himself (and his dad, I suppose). Why, he had even cut out his mother by calling himself the son of a Kansas farmer.

Raw ambition was something Brownback had in spades. As I stood there listening, my thoughts flashed back to 1995 when Brownback was diagnosed with a melanoma, and he felt he was in crisis. One night while the family was sleeping, he got out of bed and chose to reread, of all things, his resume . . . high school class president, and so on.

Without a doubt, ambition can serve a good purpose. But in politics, as in business, followers accrue most faithfully and most ardently when they sense that the leader is magnanimous and generous of spirit. For instance, it's been estimated that the emotional climate within a company may account for as much as 30% of its performance. Who predominantly creates that climate? Studies indicate that it's mostly the senior leadership.[11]

To get the most from people, leaders at every level of an organization create followers who believe that the greater "us" will feed the "me." Together they will attain more than they would on their own. How did I decide Brownback would never be a great leader? Because **great leaders have the qualities of a winner willing to share the glory and look out for the group.**

FORWARD-LOOKING: JAUNDICE-YELLOW GLASSES

It isn't enough, of course, as a leader to realize your own ambition of reaching higher office—whether that be the White House or the CEO corner-office suite. There's also the matter of what realizing that dream will mean for your supporters' future and the life they can imagine for themselves. In other words, voters and employees alike wonder: what's in it for me?

In trying to answer that essential leadership question during the 2008 primary season, the candidates instinctively gravitated to one of three distinct time periods. The first and least satisfying approach was to invoke the distant past. Thompson seemed the most prone to doing so. Based on the testing we conducted on Thompson's TV commercials, it would appear that voters couldn't tell what his point was. His vague talk of "guiding principles" from the Founding Fathers garnered no emotional response from them. A typical voter comment that reinforced the facial coding data was, "I don't get what he's saying." Well, perhaps that's because he wasn't saying very much.

Edwards' approach wasn't that much better. More so than any other major candidate, his focus was on the here-and-now. Yes, there was talk of the future. But the issue of who was currently stealing America's collective economic "pie" overshadowed any substantial vision of what lies ahead, and how people's lives will improve as a result of change.

While Thompson offered history lessons, Edwards offered grievance lessons. While Thompson safely heralded George Washington and company from long ago, Edwards was busy aggressively despising the role of lobbyists in both the recent past and present. While Thompson favored examples too distant in time to relate to easily, Edwards hardly looked forward except to promise a big cat-fight with corporate interests.

The third option was to embrace the future, a time when all problems will get solved and Americans inhabit a land of milk-and-honey. The problem is, voters have heard that before and aren't readily buying it anymore. It's been said that the Victorian Era looked at the world through rose-colored glasses. Today the trend is toward *jaundice-yellow* glasses—as exemplified by both the hunger for authenticity and Fran Leibowitz's quip: "No matter how cynical I get, it's impossible to keep up."[12]

That left McCain, promising hard times. Talk about a truly differentiated positioning among the candidates! Thompson was painting the past. Edwards was all gripes about the present. Clinton, Obama, Giuliani and Romney were all busy making vague, sweeping promises about the future, while Huckabee was simply promising to be a nice guy. McCain alone promised endless struggle.

McCain's favorite phrase might sound downright Victorian. Time and again he refers to the audience as "my friends." But his favorite theme is a combination of fighting, honor and sacrifice. And it's all steeped in military terms. Regarding Afghanistan, for example, who else among the candidates would seem almost happy to say something like, "Things will get worse before they get better"? Only McCain.

The need to "fight," to "stand up," to "take on" challenges is quintessential McCain. But at the same time, the guy can appear more intent on selling revenge instead of hope. I'm thinking of the initial Republican debate, where he described how he would chase Bin Laden to "the gates of hell." Then having said that and, apparently, realizing that he sounded like a man at least half-possessed, McCain tried to recover his composure. So he added the creakiest of social smiles to a face given to anger.

McCain is right that leadership is a tough job involving "tough choices." Moreover, he's right that leadership involves preparing people for what's likely to be down the line. But what's less certain, I think, is just how well he answers the call for the other qualities that constitute being forward-looking.

How else do great leaders stay on-emotion in looking forward? For one thing, they convey a clear vision of the future in a manner that soothes anxiety and brings relief. For another, they value being emotionally open and imaginative, exploring the situation at hand to detect patterns and trends. Then they use those abilities to create a picture of the future that followers will find vividly clear and exciting. McCain favors Ernest Hemingway novels. But maybe he should read Sigmund Freud, whose pleasure principle reminds us that **great leaders never forget to project how lives will improve as a result of change.**

INSPIRING: A GOOD BEDSIDE MANNER

Great leaders looking to do more with less should take heed of Ron Paul's campaign as an on-emotion example of how a commitment to principle can motivate followers. Among the candidates of either party consistently assigned to the second tier by the pundits, only Paul distinguished himself. Among his accomplishments was being the second most-viewed candidate on YouTube (after Obama), and raising over $34 million.[13,14]

How did Paul accomplish that? He did so first and foremost by appealing to ideals. **Great leader stress how their vision involves a move to a superior position**. Paul did that by taking an anti-IRS, anti-NAFTA, anti-IMF, anti-NATO stance. His libertarian views may have led critics in Congress to dub him "Dr. No," but his supporters love them. Never accused of being a flip-flopper, Paul rested his candidacy on the principle of freedom by advocating for a government he "mostly doesn't want to do things."

It would be hard to over-emphasize how much the Paul candidacy was driven by emotionally-laden ideas. When I ventured over to his encampment at the Ames Straw Poll, the hillside in front of it was strewn with banners. They all had quotations, like this one from President John Adams: "Fear is the foundation of most governments."

Yes, Paul was clearly a libertarian. But beyond that it wasn't easy to categorize this former small-town doctor. Gravel was really a dead-ringer for Howard Beal in *Network*, given his mad-as-hell rhetoric. Meanwhile, Tancredo spoke of "alien" invaders and was heir apparent of the 19th century, anti-immigrant Know Nothing Party. Paul alone was able to draw supporters from both the left and right wing of the political spectrum.

Here's one reason why: Paul's body language during debates was exceedingly authentic. He'd wring his hands in anguish at American foreign policy. (He used the word "empire" a lot.) When he couldn't believe what his rivals were saying, the area just below his lower lip would bulge in anger. Yes, he would also smile. But his most interesting and characteristic look was when his mouth would fall open in amazed horror at what he heard being advocated by his rivals.

Dr. Paul's Diagnosis: Empire Illness

Right up until the moment he finally conceded to McCain in mid-June, Paul was the most emotionally compelling candidate the Republicans had. In Ames, I noticed that Paul even got the Romney fans, conspicuous in their telltale yellow t-shirts, to stand and applaud him after his speech. A great leader stays on-emotion by giving people a cause that distinguishes them from others, a cause that becomes an opportunity to feel hope and pride.

"The larger campaign for freedom is just getting started," Paul said in conceding the fight to McCain. "That I promise you. We're not about to let all this good work die."[15]

POSITIVE: SUNSHINE WITHOUT WARMTH

If there was any Republican candidate who stood in starkest contrast to Paul, it would be Romney. Dr. No meets Mr. Yes. The former was as often scowling and agitated as the latter sought to convey smooth assurance. Moreover, the former was as naturally motivated by principle as the latter was aided by money—even to the point of reportedly paying some consultants $200,000 to plan how he could buy his way to victory at the Ames Straw Poll. (No wonder I overheard a Paul supporter excitedly tell a friend early in the afternoon: "The Romney money-machine buses are arriving half-empty.")

After the event was over and Romney had won (of course), *Time* magazine's Joe Klein would write that "Romney now has to be considered a strong favorite for the Republican nomination."[16] I never saw it that way. For one thing, I didn't see how Romney could prevail in a rural state. To the average Iowan, I imagine he has the look and feel of the banker who had turned down your farm loan.

Second, in contrast to Paul's efforts, Romney's directed messaging didn't feel like it was being delivered with real passion. That's certainly what we found in our testing. Among the speech excerpts my company tested, Paul's call for freedom inspired four times as much emotional response as Romney's conscientious reiteration of why he should be president. Every time I heard Romney go through his key points, his platform of strengthening . . . the family, the economy, and the military, I heard the voice of the consultants who had crafted this positioning, not the authentic voice of a passionate individual.

In short, given Romney's rationally-oriented promise of competency ("a businessman who can get the job done"), I began to think of him as akin to another Massachusetts governor who had run for president promising competency. Here was Romney, a kind of Mormon Dukakis.

Third, there was the problem of Romney's smiles, a contradiction revealed by facial coding. The candidate projected an upbeat, warm, positive personality. But when I watched him smile in debates, the sensation I felt was sunshine without warmth.

As shown by Ekman's FACS, a true smile involves the muscle around the eye relaxing, bringing tell-tale laugh lines and even a twinkle to the eye. In contrast, social smiles only involve the mouth. As such, Romney's social smiles are more akin to the grip-and-grins seen in annual reports, a photo of the CEO shaking someone's hand for the camera.

On and on, Romney as the Energizer Bunny of Social Smiles

There's another key differentiator. True smiles typically will last no more than four seconds. Social smiles can go on and on, and Romney's can set endurance records. To me, Romney became the Energizer Bunny of Social Smiles. The guy was also a politician with a huge authenticity problem.

Yes, being positive in an important emotional attribute in order to be a great leader. People follow—and pull for—people they like. So being upbeat, supportive and full of good will is vital to moving the enterprise forward. The work will flow better if buoyed by a sense of enjoyment. Moreover, **people will be less inclined to panic if they feel like victory is possible, even imminent**. At the same time, however, optimism should both feel and prove to be genuine. Otherwise, it won't work, as I am about to discuss.

TRUSTWORTHY: THE SPECTER OF NIXON

Fortunately for everyone, including leaders, there's no single muscle in the face that reveals a lie. If there were, chances are that the lines to have plastic surgery remove it would stretch around the block, making the botox fad look minor by comparison. Honesty matters because nobody ever forgets the feeling of having been told a lie. People want to lie (with impunity) but don't want to be on the receiving end. Therefore, a lack of honesty—or just the perception of a lie—is strong enough to hobble the effectiveness of leaders. Even in politics, where voters have come to expect a degree of dissembling, the label of "liar" has been the downfall of many.

Not by chance, I suspect, social smiles often emerge during a lie. That certainly seemed to be the case during the 2008 race.

On the Republican side, rivals criticized Romney for changing his position on abortion. Huckabee, for one, said of Romney, "It's hard to trust a man who reaches political puberty at the age of 60." Romney then broadened his credibility gap when he claimed to have been a hunter "pretty much all my life," only to have it revealed that he'd only been hunting twice—ever.

Among the Democrats, even Clinton's supporters harbored doubts about her veracity. In mid-December 2007, a survey by *The New York Times* and CBS, asked Democratic voters to respond to the following for the three leading candidates: "Says what believes."[17] Here's how people answered:

***New York Times/CBS* Poll Regarding Veracity**

"Which candidate says what they believe?"		
Candidate	**Iowa**	**New Hampshire**
Hillary Clinton	47%	54%
John Edwards	77%	61%
Barack Obama	82%	75%

What's responsible for Clinton's distant, third-place finish? You could point to a history that links her directly or at least tangentially, with her husband, Bill, to White Water, Travelgate, and the Monica Lewinsky saga, among other matters. Then there's her propensity to show social smiles. Those smiles are intended to broadcast happiness. But especially when mixed with flashes of contempt and anger, they instead create an impression of disingenuousness and inauthenticity.

Timing matters, too. After all, the mid-December poll came just two weeks after the first Democratic debate held in Philadelphia, moderated by the late Tim Russert and Brian Williams. The exchange that got the biggest press the next day involved Clinton's apparent flip-flop over whether illegal immigrants should be granted drivers licenses. In response, Edwards observed: "Unless I missed something, Senator Clinton said two different things in the course of about two minutes."

But in the final analysis, the driver licenses flap wasn't crucial. Unlike another issue that emerged that evening, it didn't challenge Clinton's value proposition as a candidate. The key question was really whether, and when, the Clintons would release Bill's presidential papers. She was touting her "35 years" of experience. The opportunity to read the papers would help verify the degree to which Hillary had played a significant role in his administration.

Clinton said on the air that she was in favor of the papers being released after "[the Archives] do their process" (as in, they're slow and I'm okay with that). Well, Russert wasn't buying her explanation. He'd done his homework and held up a letter from the Clintons asking for the papers to be held back until 2012. Clinton's response was to stare down Russert, believing perhaps that his inquiry couldn't really do damage.

However, Obama then added his voice. "We've just been through the most secretive administration in American history," he asserted, linking Clinton to Bush, before also challenging Clinton to release the papers. How ironic that a woman who had served as a staff member for Nixon's impeachment hearings would herself be politically harmed by secrecy surrounding presidential documents.

Obama and McCain, among others, could also be picked on here. Politicians prevaricate. But surely you get the point. In a matter of a month, Clinton went from somebody a cartoonist had depicted as Bionic Woman, throwing aside her puny male rivals, to a third-place finish in Iowa.

Nobody can afford to be judged dishonest. Why is honesty so preeminent a factor? The answer is that for most of us in life, honesty comes first. We want to know where a person stands. Therefore, leaders must protect their credibility above all else. **People follow people they like, and liars aren't well-liked** (as Clinton painfully learned).

STABILITY: FIT FOR COMMAND

Not all emotional displays are authentic. Likewise, not all instances of speaking from the heart are necessarily good to share. Here's a potential case in point.

"I'm angry this morning," said Arizona senator John McCain, and sitting where I was—no more than three feet from the man—I certainly had to agree, based on my knowledge of FACS. There are about half a dozen ways in which people can express anger on their faces, ranging from slight annoyance to a *I-can't-wait-to-kill-you* type of look. In general, anger reveals itself as a narrowing, a tightening of the muscles, like a snake coiling to strike. But, as I explained in describing every candidates' facial expressions on *Time* magazine's web site, each person is unique. So naturally McCain has his own version of anger.

In McCain's case, it's what I call his puffer fish look. His eyebrows lower and pull together, and his chin rises, pushing his mouth up into what would be a bulging, defiant version of a frown, if it wasn't for two other movements. His lips will press together tightly, even as he puffs out his cheeks in exasperation.

In that morning's town hall meeting, McCain went on to tell the audience that he was mad for a very specific reason. The topic was bridges, and the link McCain wanted to draw was between the pork-barrel "Bridge to Nowhere" in Alaska and the country's under-funded infrastructure, including, namely, the bridge that had just collapsed in Minneapolis a few days prior.

Among those on hand to hear him speak, McCain definitely had my attention. After all, I had driven under that very bridge on my commute home no more than a minute before it came down. So I was keen on McCain's critique, and yet I wanted to laugh. By then I had already been watching and facially coding him for several months. I could quantify what many other people already sense. McCain is almost *always* angry. Sometimes he's indignant. Sometimes he's impatient. Sometimes he's livid. Sometimes . . . you get the idea.

McCain has, in fact, been nicknamed "Senator Hothead" by at least one publication inside the Beltway. But the question is, does it matter? In regards to leaders, what do we know about what kind of personality is most suitable for the job?

Fortunately, a good answer exists by turning to the leading psychology model for analyzing personality. Called the "Big Five" factor model, it focuses on five broad traits of personality. Only one of them is defined negatively: neuroticism. So to make it parallel with the others, let's refer to it as stability. Being stable means you are well-adjusted, instead of being moody, tense, easily discouraged—or prone to such impulsive behavior that you get a nickname like "Senator Hothead."

Compared to stability, the other four traits are relatively mundane. There's extraversion, openness, agreeableness, and conscientious. Clearly, stability is the one to worry about most.

As shown by the table below, my company tracked down and synthesized studies to link how specific emotions correlate to the Big Five factors.[18] In other words, we wanted to learn: what's the emotional profile for a given trait? Take stability, for instance; to what degree does displaying each type of emotion make you more or less likely to be stable?

We found there's enough data to establish numerical correlations for four of the seven core emotions captured by facial coding. As a result, we discovered that stability correlates strongly to feeling happiness (a positive correlation of 4.43 on a scale of one/low to five/high). At the same time, displays of the three negative emotions for which there's data indicate that, in descending order, anger, sadness, then fear have very strong, inverse, negative correlations to stability. So someone who is rarely happy but frequently angry, sad or afraid is at much greater risk of being an unstable person.

Overall Correlation Ratings

Comparing the Big-Five Traits to Four Key Emotions

	Stability	Extraversion	Openness	Agreeableness	Conscientousness
Happiness	4.63	4.01	1.84	2.88	3.38
Sadness	(4.20)	(2.33)	(0.83)	(1.83)	(3.17)
Fear	(4.17)				
Anger	(4.56)	(2.00)	(0.33)	(3.50)	(3.67)

(5) = High Negative Correlation **High Positive Correlation = 5**

To understand which emotional displays reinforce or undermine a given trait, remember that a score of either positive or negative five indicates a perfect correlation between an emotion and the trait.

Based on correlating McCain's own admission of anger with my facial coding verification of its prevalence, what are we to conclude? Prone to anger—while lacking the emotional rudder that displays of happy smiles would provide—McCain doesn't fit the profile for stability. In fact, he's likely to be *highly unstable* and, as such, arguably not very emotionally fit to be commander in chief.

Dismiss as innuendo the rumors that were reportedly circulated in 2000 by people associated with the George Bush campaign alleging that McCain's torture and extended stay in solitary confinement in Hanoi had left him "unhinged."[19] But look at the Big Five model and our emotional correlations. You'll see that anger undermines the traits of both conscientiousness and agreeableness as well. Nevertheless, the trait most vulnerable to being undermined by displays of anger is unquestionably stability.

The bottom line here is that followers expect their leaders to be dependable, mature, self-controlled: in a word, stable. Since emotions are highly contagious, **being truly competent and fit for office means a greater propensity for displays of happiness than giving in to toxic, negative emotions.** McCain can joke about being angry. But revealed emotions are rightly taken as substance by would-be supporters who track a leader's every move—and expression—in evaluating whether they're with a winner or not.

ENEREGETIC: DROOPY DOG SYNDROME

Speaking of winning, what does it take? Besides stability, other qualities like assertiveness and resiliency also come readily to mind. Clinton showed those other qualities by competing right up until the end of the primary season. McCain has done so, too, whether as a prisoner in Vietnam or by overcoming the mid-year 2007 prediction by ABC's George Stephanopoulus that his candidacy was a case of "dead man walking."

Who represents the opposite end of the spectrum when it comes to being energetic? That would have to be Thompson. I saw him live just once, at the Iowa State Fair, where the audience sat waiting on blocks of bundled hay for the big man with the rumbling baritone to speak. When Thompson showed up in a pair of Gucci shoes, the first facial coding detail I noticed was how little the guy emoted. It was as if we in the audience were playing the role of the adoring kids, hoping for dad's attention after he had come home from work. Meanwhile, Thompson looked more like someone who would welcome a pre-dinner cocktail.

A half hour of watching the amiable but disengaged Thompson counsel his supporters to "keep their powder dry" was all it took. By then I had concluded that, more likely than not, the emotional response of Republicans to his candidacy would ultimately be boredom.

Two explanations rooted in facial coding brought me to that conclusion. The first was seeing how emotionally disengaged Thompson was himself, rarely expressive. The second was that when he did emote, it was in a low-intensity sort of way. Emotions invite reciprocity. For instance, the saying, *smile and the world smiles with you*, is really true. A smile begets a smile. In Thompson's case, he showed boredom. That's a low-grade version of disgust, signaling "no taste" instead of "bad taste." But it involves rejection all the same. In other words, I doubt that in his heart-of-hearts Thompson was really very excited about running for president.

This Tired Dog Don't Hunt

The voters we sampled felt likewise. When my company was capturing not only video for facial coding purposes but also an audio track, one man memorably said: "I wouldn't like this cat for anything; he looks old and tired." Change the type of animal, and I would agree about the level of vitality Thompson was projecting. To me he looked more like the old Droopy Dog cartoon character, lacking ambition. When I finally saw Stephanopolus in person on the campaign trail, he confirmed my diagnosis by telling me Thompson was about to drop out.

Energy level matters. In politics, business, and life in general, **we choose to ally ourselves with people who appear active and vigorous**. For example, companies know that burned-out leaders injure their prospects. So over time, they seek to identify and remove the estimated 9% of executives who are actively disengaged on the job.[20] In being so low-key, Thompson apparently forgot that to motivate others requires feeling and expressing vibrancy yourself.

ACCESSIBLE: PLAY MISTY FOR ME

Besides the emotions leaders typically display, there's one other way in which followers evaluate them. That's *occasional* displays, unrehearsed moments that may offer less guarded insights into a leader's character. Both candid camera type video, posted to YouTube, and debate highlights provide examples.

Among the Republicans, Romney had the greatest problem with spontaneity. Here's a case in point. In an early debate from Des Moines, Stephanopoulos opened by showing a Brownback TV spot attacking Romney. The ex-Massachusetts governor replied by saying one shouldn't attack fellow Republicans. Given the perfect lead-in, Stephanopoulos then played a Romney TV spot attacking Giuliani, in turn, regarding his own abortion position.

How did Romney react? In rapid succession over a span of less than two seconds, I coded him flinching, then narrowing his lips in anger, only to then close his eyes. People typically close their eyes to shield themselves, to ward off sadness.

In 2004, I had watched Wesley Clark do likewise during a surprise attack on him by a rival candidate amid a New Hampshire debate. Even more emotionally injured than Romney, Clark had also momentarily bowed his head, like a boxer stunned by a blow. My sense in 2004 was that Clark's time atop the military chain of command hadn't helped to prepare him for the give-and-take of politics. My conclusion in 2008 was that life atop the corporate ladder had also not prepared Romney well for unrehearsed interactions.

Support for that conclusion came during a 2008 New Hampshire debate. "Mike, don't characterize my position," Romney said, to which Huckabee replied: "Which one?" Romney's response was a half-squint, half-wince expression of anger, surprise, and all-around pain.

As suggested by that last exchange, clearly Huckabee was the less scripted, more accessible candidate, at ease with spontaneity. Here's a very different example. As I came off the set from an interview on Fox TV, live from Des Moines, on the eve of the Iowa caucuses, there was Huckabee. About to win—and win big—he could have easily chosen to ignore me as I strolled by him amid a circle of advisors and media types.

But he didn't. Instead, he made eye contact and gave me a nod as I passed, providing enough encouragement to approach him.

After introducing myself, I told him that for months now I'd been predicting he would rise in the polls given his affability and emotionally authentic campaigning style. What was Huckabee's response? "Just you and me, baby," he said, as he put his arm around me for a moment and grinned broadly. Looking me in the eye, he added: "Las Vegas has got me at 100 to one [odds]."

Meanwhile, among the Democrats the biggest revelation—or irony—regarding Obama was that here was somebody whose campaign so successfully inspired spontaneity from its supporters, yet rarely benefitted from displays of it from Obama himself. Yes, after losing New Hampshire Obama stood on stage and closed his eyes for a moment in a genuine display of sadness while his wife, Michelle, embraced him from behind.

But an instance like that was rare. Instead, there were other more noteworthy occasions when the candidate whose campaign was premised on hope and goodwill went seriously off-emotion, displaying emotional reactions that didn't fit his strategy.

One of those times was during the second Philadelphia debate, just prior to the Pennsylvania primary. Facing a barrage of negative, personal questions for the first 45 minutes, Obama faltered. His usual serenity was absent. Instead, that evening his mouth tightened in annoyance—even exasperation. His smiles were weak and unbelievable. Grim, glum, vexed, petulant and peevish. That was the Obama on display that evening, a candidate who even looked away from the camera at times during the debate—wanting to be above it all, above the fray, and yet still be president.

Even worse for Obama, because it was so petty, ungenerous and unnecessary, was Snubgate. That's what the media called the moment before Bush's State of the Union speech, when Obama failed to shake Clinton's hand.

"I was turning away because Claire [McCaskill] asked me a question as Senator Kennedy was reaching forward," he explained afterwards.[21] However, I trust a pair of photographs taken just before the incident. What did they show? In one, Obama's hands were tucked across his chest, eyes narrowed, lips pressed together in anger as he stood with Kennedy, while eyeing Clinton. The other photo I facially coded showed him alongside Kennedy again. Only this time he had what could only be called a gloating grin spread across his face, perhaps enjoying Kennedy's endorsement from earlier that day for the great and beneficial coup it was.

As with so much of the primary season, Obama won the nomination but Clinton provided more human drama. It was a story line I never would have anticipated early on. After all, until Iowa what Clinton showed was a steady assortment of social smiles, anger and contempt. Then the morning before the Iowa caucuses, I knew that Clinton knew she had lost when I saw her appear on *Good Morning America*. For the first time in the campaign, her social smile looked painfully forced. I saw her self-consciously lift the corners of her mouth after getting on camera. Then her smile slowly, slowly subsided, until only a shadow of it remained.

Other notable moments would follow, but New Hampshire was by far the place of the greatest emotional volatility for Clinton. Still reeling from defeat in Iowa, she found herself under attack soon afterwards in a Granite State debate when Edwards boldly declared himself and Obama agents for change—leaving out guess-who.

Clinton's response was anger—intense, prolonged anger. As she verbalized her counter-attack, her mouth was moving and open, but her lips were tight and her mouth pulled wide, forming, in effect, a funnel. Think of how a dog looks when it growls. The funnel is the strongest expression of anger, and this was the only time I saw it from *any* candidate during the primary season. As such, it's indicative of the indignity she may have felt, having been in politics all her life as a reformer only to be now excluded from those ranks by Edwards.

That wasn't all. At another point during the debate, I noticed Clinton show bitterness. The corners of her mouth and lower lip dipped downwards in a sign of disgust. To me as a facial coder, it was an expression that made her look old and sour. Seeing it, I thought to myself: *another week of that look and you can write the campaign off for sure.*

That being said, there was also the moment in that debate when Clinton rose to the occasion. She was asked whether a perceived lack of likeability was hurting her electability. "Well, that hurts my feelings," she replied in reference to the question's assumption, "but I'll try to go on." Then in a girlish tone in voice, she went on to say of Obama: "He's very likeable. I agree with that," followed by, "I don't think I'm that bad."

Now, that was a moment Clinton handled with grace, far better than most people could. But as political theatre, it paled in comparison to the big event. I'm referring of course to the famous misty-eyed moment in the diner in Portsmouth, New Hampshire.

Asked a question about how she remained so "upbeat and wonderful," by a woman amid a group of 16 undecided female voters, Clinton, voice cracking, said, "This is very personal for me. It's not just political. It's not just public." That was part one of Clinton's response, followed by a pause during which another woman chimed to obscure the awkwardness of such a public display of emotions with the supportive question: "Who does your hair?"

Part two was Clinton's recovery of composure, followed by a slight relapse. "It's not easy. It's not easy," Clinton went on to say. "And I couldn't do it if I just didn't, you know, passionately believe it was the right thing to do." Then the roller-coaster went down and back up again. After a couple of pauses, her voice softer and breaking slightly, her eyes growing just a bit misty, Clinton added: "I just don't want us to fall backwards."

Part three was Clinton returning to battle mode, back in form. Implicitly attacking Obama, she brought the moment back to the on-message pronouncement: "But some of us are right and some of us are wrong. Some of us are ready and some of us are not."

Were those *tears* and, if so, were they real? Was Clinton authentically emoting—or not? As I said in my critique for *The Politico*, the answer was mixed.[22] Yes, there were aspects that were true, especially the first part. She's not that great of an actor, after all. What was credible? There were *breaks* in her voice, *pauses* while she was looking for the right word, *pitch*-perfect emotional anguish, a *hand clinch* that looked like it was really an attempt to keep her emotions in check, and the *glistening eyes*. That's a lot to orchestrate, even for someone as capable as Clinton. So I would have to give her the benefit of the doubt in part one.

All but the end of part one and part two were quite different. Part three was especially different. True sadness brings empathy. But the words being spoken in part three didn't fit that script. Her comments were hard, accusatory and judgmental. In short, what I noticed in this case was a reversal of the usual say/feel gap: here the words told the real story as much or more than the body language.

Clinton went on to upset Obama in New Hampshire. But we never really saw the more vulnerable, accessible Clinton again during the campaign, despite her telling CNN's John Roberts: "I actually have emotions."[23] Here's why not.

Getting ready to run for the highest office in America, Clinton took her advice from chief strategist, Mark Penn. Others within her circle of advisors were advocating that she should present herself as a leader with decades of experience creating a village, working on behalf of children and families. The profile they favored was Clinton as empathetic, approachable.

What was Penn's response? "Being human is overrated,"[24] he said. Strength was the key. To him, the hurdle of a woman assuming the mantle of commander-in-chief required putting the focus squarely on ruggedness and resume, ready from day one. Clinton agreed, and so crucial months passed on the campaign trail before she concluded that Penn's strategy was wrong and dismissed him.

Leaders take heed to close the emotional gap between themselves and followers. If people don't see a leader as a real person, someone to whom they can relate, creating a collective emotional "us" is in jeopardy. People want to be able to identify with their leaders and believe their leaders care about them. Penn's strategy rested on a false dichotomy. **Convey both competency and caring.** A leader who people both respect and feel emotionally aligned with is someone they will commit to all the more.

CONCLUSION

Being on-emotion as a leader requires both savvy and dexterity. Obama and Huckabee had the best true smiles in the field, and in the primary season they both instinctively sought not to overplay that hand by flashing those smiles too often, thereby over using them and surrendering the power of authenticity. In debates, they exhibited a stance of concern, concluding that worry was frankly more on-emotion given the issues the country faces.

For our pair of social smilers, Clinton and Romney, the pursuit of being on-message came at the expense of being genuinely on-emotion in all but a few instances. Halfway to spontaneity after her first win, Clinton subsequently reverted to her comfort zone: rationality. With a different candidate and a different strategic advisor than Penn, leveraging the connection she made in New Hampshire with voters could have been a pathway to a warmer, more personable campaign. But projecting strength, not warmth, remained the Clinton campaign's goal. That's true in part because, as one of her top advisors later admitted, "she didn't understand what happened in New Hampshire."[25]

Among the candidates given to negative emotions, McCain was the only one who prospered. There's a lesson in that. Namely, how hard it is to build a supportive coalition when what people are looking for most of all is reassurance. Happiness is hardly McCain's forte. He challenges people rather than promises them a comfortable future. But aided by a life story whose narrative of suffering as a Vietnamese captive lent both credibility and purpose to his flashes of anger, McCain, though lacking in stability, found a way to break through based on projecting confidence, honesty and vitality.

3 BRANDING

Candidate as Positioned Brand

OVERVIEW

Among the candidates seeking the White House in 2008, none has proved better at branding than Obama. He started early. For one thing, at the age of 33 he published a 400-page memoir, *Dreams from My Father*, as a de facto act of branding himself. More fundamentally, in being born bi-racial, half-white and half-black in a predominantly white society, where historically even a single drop of black blood has meant a person is regarded as African-American, Obama has had to develop his own identity and, in effect, create his own "us."

As a result, Obama has very consciously struggled to belong. He's sought to be "rooted," he says, in the African-American community while also being "more than that."[1] Given a lifetime of seeking a balance, is it any wonder that Obama might readily grasp the importance of authenticity? Or worry about whether he's seen as more of an icon than an individual.

Clearly, navigating his identity and place in society all his life has prepared Obama well for branding his candidacy. In profound ways, the key objectives involved in branding should be familiar to him. On a strategic level, they consist of building a brand that's **exclusive**, **reflective**, **promising**, **aspirational**, **faithful**, **adaptive**, and **gender-sensitive**. Moreover, in writing two books Obama has shown a literary flair for the tactical aspects of branding: being **personable**, **narrative** and **imagistic**. (For a full description of these branding objectives, see Appendix B.)

Soon I will show how stories from the campaign trail illuminate each of those objectives. But first let's set the stage by showing how voters responded to all the candidates by name, which is to say to their respective brands, based on the emotions voters showed on their faces while discussing each candidate.

VOTER REACTIONS TO THE CANDIDATES

Nothing is less tangible and, therefore, more purely emotional than branding. What is the essence of branding, after all, if not inspiring a *feeling* of loyalty? Nevertheless, the instinct of so many pundits and pollsters is to emphasize the tangible issues of the day. What's wrong with that approach? Ironically enough, it's not very real. Issues change or are too complex, and voters know that politicians don't necessarily wield that much control over them anyway.

Secondly, the issues don't drive election outcomes. As George Marcus writes in the *American Political Science Review*, "It is striking that issue appraisals have little apparent direct influence on voting. Feelings about candidates, rather than thoughtful assessments regarding public policies, appear to be central to the voters' choices."[2] I agree. Less than 5% of voter comments or expressed preferences in our testing were based on so-and-so's stance regarding a variety of issues.

Our testing of how voters responded emotionally to the candidates, as individual brands, came early in the primary season, between August and October 2007. That's before most candidates' brands were very well established. Nevertheless, the data at least offers a sense of where the candidates were starting from, and who did best in lifting and transforming their brands.

The results below are based on giving voters 30 seconds in which to explain their reaction to each candidate running for their party's nomination. Then, while the voters appear on video giving their responses, we're busy facially coding their non-verbally expressed preferences. In this case, the candidates are ranked from high to low, by party, based on the percentage of values whose predominate emotional response was positive regarding their candidacies. (*See* Appendix E for further explanation.)

What's noteworthy is, contrary to accepted wisdom, familiarity doesn't breed contempt. Rather, it fosters comfort with what's known and thus more readily accepted. Having a big (familiar, engaging) brand story is of decisive importance in winning elections. As these results show, Giuliani, Clinton, and McCain started with an edge. Meanwhile, aided by their rivals' brand errors and their own strengths, Obama and Huckabee would soon make up lots of ground from relatively weak starting points.

Voter Responses to Democratic Candidates

Candidate	Positive	Neutral	Negative
Democratic Avg.	4%	3%	93%
Hillary Clinton	17%	4%	79%
Barack Obama	8%	3%	89%
John Edwards	6%	3%	92%
Bill Richardson	4%	3%	93%
Dennis Kucinich	0%	8%	92%
Joe Biden	0%	0%	100%
Christopher Dodd	0%	0%	100%
Mike Gravel	0%	0%	100%

These results indicate the percentage of voters classified as having been either positive, neutral or negative in their feelings about the various candidates; Clinton enjoys a two-for-one advantage over Obama in terms of emotional endorsement. As is true with the Republicans, however, clearly no candidate had endeared him or herself to even the party faithful.

Voter Responses to Republican Candidates

Candidate	Positive	Neutral	Negative
Republican Avg.	9%	6%	85%
Rudy Giuliani	22%	10%	68%
John McCain	13%	3%	84%
Sam Brownback	13%	13%	75%
Fred Thompson	12%	12%	76%
Mitt Romney	9%	6%	84%
Mike Huckabee	0%	8%	92%
Ron Paul	0%	0%	100%
Tom Tancredo	0%	0%	100%

On balance, Republicans felt twice as good about their candidates heading into the late fall of 2007. Besides the two big names (Giuliani and McCain), Brownback was aided by his well-known opposition to abortion and Thompson by media buzz about his candidacy.

PROMISING: THE PROBLEM WITH "INVINCIBILITY"

Being a front-runner wasn't a good place to be during the long 2008 primary season. Ask Clinton, who started her campaign with the announcement, "I'm in, and I'm in to win." Or Giuliani, whose payroll of full-time staffers numbered well over two hundred at a time when McCain was down to practically himself and his wife, Cindy.[3]

Lazy like a fox or perhaps simply lazy, Thompson waited to declare his candidacy. Testing the waters, he called it. His prognosis? The water was feeling pretty "warm." But he hesitated so long that Jay Leno couldn't help but joke: "Aren't you getting kind of wrinkly?"

Romney showed no such hesitation. He was in, full speed ahead. His strategy was all about invincibility. By spending lots of money in Iowa and New Hampshire, he hoped to win big early and build momentum. For him and Giuliani, the results from New Hampshire were crushing.[4]

It's hard to project yourself as the inevitable, electable winner when you're not winning.

Giuliani's response was weak. "We've lulled our opponents into a false sense of confidence," he lamely joked. Nobody was laughing. Romney's response may have been ever weaker, for, despite his being the businessman in the race, it suggested he didn't understand branding very well.

His concessionary speech opened with a line about winning "another silver." Meant to invoke brand story associations with his work on the 2002 Olympics, it didn't work or help his cause. After all, in getting a silver medal, so to speak, he'd spent lots of gold: something like a 20 to one ratio in losing to Huckabee in Iowa, while outspending McCain by better than two to one in New Hampshire.[5,6]

A great brand is a myth perched atop functional attributes that deliver on the brand promise and make the story feel like reality. Romney's brand story line was that at Bain & Company, and elsewhere, he was a success story, a highly competent businessman come to save America from itself. But if he couldn't save himself, how much was the guy's consulting skills worth on behalf of U.S.A., Inc.?

In essence, the problem with positioning based on inevitability is that it's a myth too easily exposed. What Romney and many of his fellow business leaders may not realize is that branding is 200-proof emotionality. If a brand delivers emotionally, myth is transformed into reality. Romney tied his strategy to delivering rationally instead, based on voting results from the early-round states.

A brand is hard to start, hard to establish, and, once in place, difficult to dislodge. But if faith gets broken, it's an epic lie and quick plunge. **Never set yourself up for failure by positioning your brand on a basis whereby faith in it can easily be punctured**. A brand is a myth. Stay mythical. One of Romney's crucial mistakes is that he made his brand too easily subject to a reality-test.

IMAGISTIC: AND NOW IN THIS CORNER . . . BABY FACE

In time, Clinton settled on her brand persona, her mask, her way of presenting herself to voters. She was a fighter, allegedly on behalf of people and not just her own ambition. That role felt right. After all, as a young girl Clinton was bullied by another girl in the neighborhood. "There's no room in this house for cowards," her mother had told her. So Clinton went back and hit the bigger girl smack in the face, knocking her down, and then ran home to proclaim, "I can play with the boys now."[7]

That's the kind of opponent McCain expected and longed for.

As a former amateur boxer in the U.S. Navy, McCain is himself pugilistic to his very core. John Weaver knows him well, having served as McCain's chief strategist. Among his assessments is this one: "There's no bar fight he will walk away from."[8] So I can only imagine how easily McCain would have related to fighting Clinton in the general election.

Instead, first Clinton (expecting Edwards to be her chief rival), then McCain (preferring Clinton), have each found themselves surprised to be up against Obama. What must have struck them about this opponent, who fights not through words so much as brand imagery instead?

For starters, Obama is audacious. Despite a cool demeanor, nobody should doubt his competitive nature and ambition. Given a chance to write a book about his status as the first African-American to head the *Harvard Law Review*, Obama instead told the publisher he wanted to write the memoir.

Then there's his face. For Obama it serves as the first, foremost and *transparent* element on which his brand is based (unlike Clinton's at times *classified* White House experience). It's a clean, fresh seemingly open face. The British author George Orwell has said that by the age of fifty, a man has the face he deserves. But here is Obama at 46, looking easily a decade younger, eternally boyish.

In fact, when Obama first moved to Chicago from Harvard Law School to begin work as an organizer, south-side residents took to calling him "Baby Face" because he looked so young.[9] Years later, Biden would trip himself up, calling Obama "articulate, bright and clean,"

(*clean*, as in not *dirty*?) adding "fresh" the next day in a hapless attempt to overcome his faux pas.

Such youthfulness—and the risk to the country of such inexperience, even naiveté—remains a big hurdle for the Obama brand. There have been references to him as the 46-year-old Virgin, and at the Martin Luther King Day rally in South Carolina, both Clinton and Edwards emphasized Obama's youth. But her reference to Obama as "an extraordinary, *young* African-American" and Edwards calling him a "talented *young* man" didn't rerail him.[10]

The role of on-emotion branding helps to explain why. Yes, there's the rational, intellectual alibi to guard Obama's cause. Anyone can point out the fact that Bill Clinton was 46 years old when he took office, and John F. Kennedy was only 43. But the real defense against the lack of stature the charge of youth posed is to wrap oneself, as Obama has done, in a series of historical hot-button associations that paint an imagistic, compelling picture in the mind's eye.

A Trio of Youthful Democrats

Did anyone say a Clinton presidency would be like "rolling the dice?"
Not that I know. But it didn't keep Bill Clinton from fretting and fuming about Obama's candidacy on *The Charlie Rose Show.*

For starters, there's the irony that while Clinton holds Bobby Kennedy's old Senate seat from New York state, Obama works in the Senate, making use of Bobby Kennedy's old Senate desk. Then there's the branding battle that raged between Bill Clinton and Ted Kennedy, both intent in their ways on branding Obama. For the former president, that effort amounted to trying to label Obama as only a minority politician who was, therefore, a minor presidential candidate, Jesse Jackson reborn. For a former president's brother, the mentoring response was to put Obama into the brand realm of John F. Kennedy.

Heady stuff that last move. But Obama had already long ago been at work building his brand on his own, through associations and the images they evoke.

There was Obama declaring his candidacy in Springfield, Illinois, where another lanky politician, Abraham Lincoln, had given his famous "House Divided" speech. There was also the frequency with which Obama cited Martin Luther King, Jr., notably his "fierce urgency of now" phrase.

Now, seeking to activate those kinds of associations may not seem like much. It might even appear obvious and easy. But if so, consider for instance what kind of brand Edwards tried to build. The personal story he chose to tell time and again focused on his being a millworker's son, who had worked long, hard, faithful hours so his boy could realize his potential.

That's fine. But the first problem with the story was that it was an old story, with declining emotional impact. The mill industry is an old-economy story; the sector is declining, going off-shore. It's a story of losing, not winning, and it involves fewer and fewer people all the time. The socio-economic trends don't support it.

Second, in focusing the story around his father, Edwards created a brand story lacking stature. It was a small story. As good a man as Edwards' humble father appears to be, *where* were some bigger hot-button associations, some labor leaders whose words we heard in the way Obama incorporates King? In short, there were no heroes in Edwards' pantheon. There was nothing to compete with the thundering oratory of someone like King still resonating in the collective ear of America, as an iconic figure, even after all these years.

In determining who would be Clinton's primary rival, it wasn't a fair fight. At an associative level, what came to mind for people? It was an image fight in which Obama could implicitly pit King and the Kennedys against media stories about Edwards' $400 haircuts and his house of 28,800 square feet, complete with a full basketball court and a roofed-in pool.

There are lessons here for anyone interested in branding.

First, don't be a blank slate, as Edwards was. Create the patterns, the associations and signature imagery you want to be known by. Make it vivid—so it sticks. Second, use repetition. What we've seen predisposes us to what we can and likely will see the next time around. Referencing Lincoln, King and Kennedy creates associations that grow weighty if reinforced.

Most of all, **remember that a brand whose name doesn't invoke mental imagery is in trouble**. Half the brain is devoted to processing visuals. That's too much real estate, and too many wasted opportunities to connect with voters and consumers alike for anybody interested in success to forego.

NARRATIVE: WHEN SMALL ISN'T BIG

Handicapping the Republican race, former Pennsylvania senator Rick Santorum would despair: "O.K., Romney can't win, Huckabee can't win, McCain can't win, Giuliani can't win—the dynamic is you have a bunch of candidates who can't win. I don't see how we don't come down to a convention that is going to decide this thing."[11] And that was *afte*r the New Hampshire primary had begun to narrow the field.

In reality, the race was decided a lot earlier than that.

In executing a campaign, think small these days. Invite people in. Strive for intimacy. Work from the ground up, using social networking to let supporters connect with one another. But when it comes to brand story status, size matters. Significance matters. Degree of relevance matters. Big is better than small, and big turning into small—as happened to Giuliani, when Biden turned his signature 9/11 leadership into something of a joke—is really nothing less than a branding disaster.

Brand Story Status Concerns

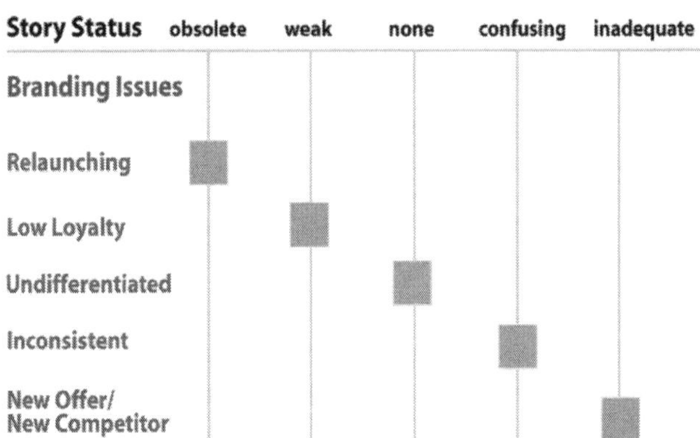

As in business, so in politics: there's always a correlation between the issues you face and why your brand's story status isn't helping you. For example, if your brand is seen as *inconsistent*, it's because your story is *confusing* and needs to be simplified and made more coherent.

Let's handicap the race a different way, using brand story size as the yardstick.

Romney's brand story lacked size and stature and was *weak*, reflective of, and reinforcing, *low loyalty*. As the CEO of American Motors, his father had enjoyed a big, strong story thanks to giving Americans both the Rambler and the phrase, "gas-guzzler." But Romney's leadership at Bain & Company didn't occupy such a prominent place in people's lives or minds. Nor did rescuing the Salt Lake City Olympics help enough, since it also reinforced his profile as belonging to a minority, Mormon religion. So count him out.

Thompson? His brand story looked big to some people early on, but was actually small. *New* to the race when he finally, officially declared his candidacy, his brand story soon proved to be *inadequate*. Remember that once upon a time, Thompson, as a not-yet-declared candidate, was nevertheless running second in the national polls based on . . . who knows what? A longing for the second coming of Reagan was the favored explanation.

However, the columnist George Will was already aptly comparing Thompson, not to Reagan, but to the Dutch tulip bulb mania of the 17th century. His reasoning? That's when the prices rose crazily high on expectations lacking substance and sustainability.[12]

In short, Thompson's bubble of support said more about Republican anxiety about the rest of the field than it did about the merits of Thompson as a future president. Soon I would see a political cartoon with a couch potato watching the ex-Senator on TV and saying to himself: "He's like REAGAN! Minus the ideology, ambition, passion, charisma, and hair."

Then there was Huckabee. As if looking like Jim Nabors and having a last name redolent of Ozark hillbillies wasn't enough of a problem, his signature biographical detail only compounded the problem. Branding is tough when the most famous thing about you is having lost 110 pounds (in response to being diagnosed with type 2 diabetes). That's because the same is true of Jared, the guy in the Subway commercials—only he's not running to become President of the United States of America.

So count out Huckabee as well. Like Thompson, his was a *new* offer saddled with an *inadequate* brand story.

From the get-go, that left McCain and Giuliani as, in reality, the only two viable contenders. Of them, the candidate with the biggest, best, most sustainable brand story was McCain. Even way down in the national polls as he was in the summer of 2007, McCain couldn't be easily counted out. The guy still enjoyed big brand equity thanks to his Hanoi Hilton experience and vast name recognition thanks to the media buzz surrounding his quixotic challenge of Bush's juggernaut in 2000.

The good news for the McCain political brand was that the guy is an authentic war hero. His is the story of a soldier who refused early, preferential dismissal from prison despite being the son of the commanding general of the American navy's Pacific fleet during his time in "Hanoi Hilton." Talk about honor.

Moreover, there is additional substance to the story given the specific details of McCain's war experience: the five and a half years in a

North Vietnamese prison, with 31 months in solitary confinement, not to mention being tortured so badly he tried to commit suicide. In the end, McCain was left permanently crippled. The great courage required to survive that experience few of us can imagine, much less match.

Republican Warriors

May 24, 1973: Lieutenant Commander McCain shakes President Nixon's hand after his five-year P.O.W. ordeal.

Meanwhile, as "America's Mayor," the single most famous hero on and after 9/11, Giuliani also enjoyed brand story size. The photo was the key. Someone had captured the mayor trying to breathe through soot and ash of Biblical proportions as he rushed to the rescue of the survivors of the collapsed Twin Towers in lower Manhattan.

The photo was such an authentic testament to Giuliani's moment of greatest valor that it could—and did—serve as the campaign's unofficial signature brand image. Like the equally famous photo of a bandaged McCain lying in a hospital in Hanoi shortly after he was shot down, it conveyed fortitude nobody could question. That is, until Giuliani overplayed his hand, often mentioning the tragedy in speeches and debates despite his only rarely visiting the 9/11 site (according to a clean-up official).

As a result, Biden felt free to criticize the ex-mayor, joking on national TV that every sentence out of Giuliani's mouth consisted of "a noun, a verb and 9/11." And because that was true, Giuliani's brand story size shriveled.

The morale here is that a brand story must be rich enough to engage people as well as strong enough to have staying power. The needs and wants (the *emotivations*) it draws on, should be as eternal and sustaining as possible. Safety remains the bottom line for everyone, a matter of survival. But the longer the timeframe expanded away from the events of 9/11, the more the immediacy of Giuliani's story faded and the more he reacted by trying to pump it back up.

Keeping a brand's narrative alive and intact depends, in part, on constantly monitoring its on-emotion relevance. In Giuliani's case, over-leveraging an increasingly stale story made it less sacred, more vulnerable to derision.

PERSONABLE: IF HE'S "JUDAS," THEN YOU MUST BE...

God knows, there were many strange days during the emotionally charged Democratic primary battle. But among the top contenders must be the day former President Bill Clinton's political advisor, James Carville, denounced Richardson as "Judas" for endorsing Obama after he dropped out of the race.

Taken literally, Carville's analogy hardly qualified as authentic. The scale and content were all wrong. His point was, of course, that Richardson was a traitor, having formerly served in Bill Clinton's administration and, therefore, apparently, expected to endorse Hillary Clinton instead of Obama. But Carville's Biblical analogy was breathtakingly grandiose. If Richardson really was Judas in this case, then wasn't Clinton, um, Christ? And wouldn't that be kind of a big stretch for even a former first lady and senator to assume?

Moreover, Carville's analogy was off-emotion. It smacked of both spiteful revenge and nervousness. It made Clinton look small and scared. After all, the analogy gave Richardson a status he would never enjoy otherwise. Who was Richardson? Having seen him give speeches, I would have say that the guy's more like Ralph Kramden from the classic TV show *The Honeymooners* than anything else.

Separated at Birth

Physical similarities between Jackie Gleason (left) and New Mexico Governor Richardson (right) get the comparison going. But it's the mannerisms of Gleason's *Honeymooner* character, Ralph Kramden, that bring the comparison home.

My frankly more apt analogy is rooted in observation, not revenge. In one of the Democratic debates, Richardson was asked why he had been so slow to call for his fellow Hispanic, Alberto Gonzalez, to step down as Bush's Attorney General. Well, it took Richardson forever to answer the question—and he never really did.

In facially coding Richardson as he struggled to reply, I suddenly saw Jackie Gleason's old character role revived. There was the blustering, the hemming and hawing, the shrugging of the shoulders that Gleason's Kramden character exhibits on the show.

To continue *this* analogy, consider Kramden's wife, the very fine actress Audrey Meadows. Her role on *The Honeymooners* was to take none of Kramden's guff. She could see right through his blustering. She was neither impressed nor intimidated—in the very same way Clinton wasn't worried about Richardson's role as a rival candidate. Richardson was no threat to her, but in dropping out of the race not much of an opportunity, either. In truth, his endorsing of Obama was mostly a sign of trouble, a disaffirmation of Clinton's candidacy and her chances of reaching the White House, as well as some opportunism on Richardson's part.

What kind of branding lesson can be taken from Begala's emotionally-charged, silly and inappropriate comparison? It's this. Both in politics and business, **have a personable brand people can relate to plausibly**. Clinton as Christ was implausible at best, and offensive and ludicrous at worst. The analogy distracted from the branding task of making Clinton someone voters could simultaneously admire and relate to well.

A great brand character isn't pompous, generic or distant. Instead, that role should help to make the brand/customer relationship feel like a close friendship or a really good marriage, a sharing of outlook, values and experiences.

Speaking of married life, give Romney credit for the funniest, most genuinely self-effacing joke I heard during the campaign. It goes like this. Apparently, one day he asked his wife, Ann, "Did you ever in your wildest dreams believe I would be running for president?" Her reply: "You weren't in my wildest dreams." So to clarify, have a *vivid* brand personality that doesn't involve a big stretch (unlike Carville's). It should be just enough of a stretch to keep things both interesting and plausible.

FAITHFUL: THE ADVANTAGE OF BEING BULLET-PROOF

Quite possibly, the day McCain won his party's nomination no votes were even cast. The occasion was the debate held in Florida on November 29th, 2007. There the inevitability of McCain's attack on Romney crystalized. And it happened over an issue on which the Arizona senator is absolutely bullet-proof: prisoner torture. When Romney refused to rule out the use of water-boarding as a means of interrogating terrorist suspects, McCain couldn't hold back. "I'm astonished . . . that anyone could believe it's not torture," he muttered, glaring at his opponent.

Romney's response was to grin nervously.

I for one felt the hairs on my neck rise on witnessing the exchange. Here McCain knew unequivocally what he was talking about, and his anger was suitably on-emotion—even laudatory. Moreover, it would be followed by another emotional response that made McCain look even more like a principled, tough-minded humanitarian.

Still mistakenly thinking the other was his primary barrier to getting the nomination, Giuliani and Romney were battling it out regarding illegal immigration. *As mayor, my opponent was running a "sanctuary city,"* charged Romney. *My opponent has enjoyed a "sanctuary mansion,"* Giuliani retorted, alluding to the status of some of the ground crew at work on Romney's home.

For his part, Thompson was effective. He dryly said of Romney's former support for an immigration bill like the one no longer acceptable, "Now, he's taken another position, surprisingly."

But it was McCain and Huckabee who really rose to the occasion. First, McCain interjected: "This whole debate saddens me a bit." Then Huckabee, who as governor of Arkansas had, like McCain, expended political capital seeking to take a moderate, compromise position on this inflammatory issue, stepped in. Rejecting the notion that children of illegal immigrants should be barred from state scholarship programs. Huckabee turned to Romney and said: "In all due respect, we are a better country than to punish children for what their parents did."

The reaction was immediate, at least as gauged by David Broder's subsequent editorial. "If the Republican Party really wanted to hold on to the White House in 2009," he wrote, "It's clear what it would do. It would grit its teeth, swallow its doubt, and nominate a ticket of John McCain for president and Mike Huckabee for vice-president—and president-in-waiting."[13]

Broder's checklist in support of that verdict sounded to me a lot like a defense of authenticity: "clarity, character and simple humanity." Months ago, in observing Huckabee's body language and style of interacting with voters at the Ames Straw Poll, I had seen his potential. Here now was Broder coming to a similar conclusion—even to the point of likewise suggesting that the former Baptist pastor would make a good vice presidential choice.

Despite political pressures to indulge in rhetoric about illegal immigration, two candidates proved to be faithful to the essence of their brand values, **preserving integrity, which is essential if a brand is going to survive long-term.** Giuliani and Romney pandered in the here-and-now. In contrast, McCain and Huckabee stuck with their perspective roles, the noble warrior defending human dignity and the pastor tending the flock.

ASPIRATIONAL: EDWARDS & THE GREEK CHORUS

In retrospect, it strikes me and perhaps many others that Edwards would have made a far better Democratic general election nominee and campaigner in 2004 than John Kerry. My favorite, on-emotion political cartoon from that year's race showed Kerry as the Frankenstein monster, strapped to an operating table, with electric shock being applied thanks to the jumper cables also attached to the corners of Edwards' huge smile. The point was that Edwards was simply so much more upbeat and full of vitality than the morose and stilted Kerry.

But in the 2008 race, happiness just seemed so retro. Or so it would appear. Certainly, Edwards had become more somber. What had changed? Perhaps the man, given most notably the diagnosis of terminal cancer his wife received just as the new campaign was getting going.

Then again maybe his darker mood was simply a case of political calculation. There was at least one observer who felt that Edwards had decided to position himself more aggressively. As Peter Leyden, Director of the New Politics Institute, explained it: "Edwards is swinging for the fences. He's got strategy reasons for doing that—he's got to get on the board differently."[14] Edwards' decision to propose more sweeping policy recommendations was the rational part of that strategy. *Anger* was the emotional part.

There proved to be two major problems with that aspect of Edwards' brand strategy, however. First, anger wasn't unique as an emotional platform. Second, it proved to be mostly off-emotion when it came to inspiring voters to support his campaign.

Let's return to the first problem. If anybody was most hurt by the crowded Democratic field, that person was Edwards'. In a sea of white male faces, he alone among the three major contenders failed to stand out. By gender Clinton and by skin tone Obama were clearly differentiated—and on truly historic terms—being the first viable female and African-American candidates for the highest office in the country.

Edwards & the Greek Chorus of Anger

Edwards towered over the others—Biden, Dodd, Kucinich and Gravel—in voter preference surveys. But all of these candidates were angry and ultimately doomed.

Moreover, Edwards faced the problem that four of his rivals—Dodd, Biden, Kucinich, and Gravel—formed a Quartet of Grumpy Old Men, a sort of Greek Chorus of Anger. (Or if you want to take the polling numbers into account, you could think of this group as Edwards and the four dwarfs.)

Yes, what Edwards had on all of the Greek Chorus members, with perhaps the slight exception of Kucinich, was youth. But such a preponderance of anger made it a *commodity*, rather than a differentiator. Put another way, the crowded field hurt Edwards the most because, as an emotional brand platform, his angry-white-man approach blurred with others.

Besides, if he—and they—started out as angry, where was there to go? How did you top it? What was the next level? *The apocalypse*?

The second problem with Edwards' brand strategy was that it wasn't going to create a longing for membership among potential supporters. Edwards' anger fit a populist battle cry attacking big oil, big pharmaceutical companies, big insurance companies, corporate lobbyists, and the like. Overall, Edwards was after the "powerful insiders" who he says have "rigged the system."

As a critique, it's got merit. But in emotional brand terms, it led to the following conundrum. How aspirational was Edwards' mixture of anger and attacks if it assumes that Americans are a bunch of victims?

A strong brand takes a little bolder position that its rivals do. It's not *average*. Edwards might have achieved that brand goal if it hadn't been for the Greek Chorus. Moreover, the positioning must be readily perceivable and important to people. Edwards did fairly well there. But what he didn't handle nearly as well was the aspirational, dream aspect of branding. A brand should speak to people's innate, evolutionary desire to impress others, to feel special, and worthy of affinity.

To that end, **a great brand story makes people want to say "we" and "us" when talking about it.** Unfortunately the Edwards' pitch could be seen as telling Americans: you've lost. Take away hope and what did the Edwards brand offer? Nothing that would cause voters to feel like the Edwards' candidacy was a bridge to a larger community affirming who they want to be.

REFLECTIVE: WAY TOO PRETTY IN PINK

If there was a major candidate who fell most afoul of the key branding rule that you should always mirror your customers' beliefs, Giuliani qualifies. Undercutting his prospects for the White House were many problems, starting with his status as a "three-time divorcee." As my company's 2007 study of bias had revealed, up to two-thirds of American voters may be reluctant to vote for a guy who seemed to have spent a lifetime exchanging wives.

In essence, shifting alliances and lack of consistency was Giuliani's downfall. The mayor had been a Democrat until 1980, and in the words of former Republican State Island borough president Guy Molinari, "The only thing that makes sense is that he becomes a Democrat [again]."[15] Pro-choice, pro-gun control, pro gay rights, Giuliani was fundamentally at odds with the issues agenda of the religious right wing commonly believed capable of making or breaking a Republican nominee.

Moreover, Giuliani's brand associations weren't nearly as compact and coherent as McCain's. His rival could summon up an entire set of images and vocabulary centered around such staples as uniforms, honor, duty, and service to one's country.

Against that, what did Giuliani have? The answer was a brand story with a few odd chapters. More specifically, in this case I'm talking about a couple of photographs nearly as famous as those from 9/11. One was of his Honor dressed in drag as Marilyn Monroe, sauntering in pink chiffon at a mayoral press conference. The other was again of him dressed in drag, this time in fishnet stockings, as he danced at New York City's Radio Hall with the Rockettes.

In addition, the array of facial expressions that Giuliani was capable of—including mock fear and surprise—spoke to another problem with Giuliani's brand image. His personality and actions are rooted in a persistent duality.

All politicians have something of a stage persona, denoting the face they choose to show the public. But in Giuliani's case, there's a theatrical sensibility to him that goes beyond the norm. In hitting the campaign trail, America's Mayor had tried to trade growls for smiles. That I could plainly see. But it was the man's underlying psychology, his oddball nature, I wondered about most.

Over time, I dubbed Giuliani the Broadway Priest. The Broadway part was easy given Giuliani's New York City roots. Like Huckabee, he thrives in being on stage, in the public eye, with an (adoring) audience. As a boy, he had listened to Italian operas and devoured Winston Churchill's speeches, as if already projecting larger-than-life roles for himself. Years later, Jimmy Breslin would famously say of Giuliani that he was "a small man in search of a balcony."[16]

Whether that was really a fair comment or not, one thing was certain: Giuliani could do theatre. During the debates, he would prove to have by far the greatest expressive, emotional range of any of the Republican candidates. That emotional dexterity, even showboat quality, made for good television. In another candidate, it might have been okay. But Giuliani's dexterity can border on the bizarre, the difference between a gymnast and a contortionist.

A case in point would be his speech to the National Rifle Association. During it, he took a phone call from his wife, Judith, telling her, in what some observers considered to be a staged stage whisper: "I love you, and I'll give you a call as soon as I'm finished, O.K.?"[17]

Such gamesomeness seemed all the odder given the second part of Giuliani's dual nature. After all, the other part of the label I gave Giuliani was Priest, and that part also really never wavered.

Time and again, what struck me as well as others about the Mayor was how moralizing he was. Whether the enemy consisted of squeegee men, graffiti artists, loiters, prostitutes, or organized crime, Giuliani always sought to prosecute. What was the compulsion to do so?

It wouldn't take a psychologist to stress that Giuliani's father, Harold, had been arrested for armed robbery in Manhattan at the age of 26 and spent time in prison.[18] Could it be that Giuliani's career of chasing down criminals was really a private war with his father? As told to me by the girlfriend of a Giuliani campaign aide, "Broadway Priest" was, indeed, accurate, given how Giuliani tells friends he knows he will be going to hell for his sins.

The long and short of it, in terms of Giuliani's brand was its consistent duality. Consider for instance how he tried to have it both ways regarding abortion. In reference to Roe vs. Wade, he would say in one debate, "It would be O.K. to repeal. Or it would be O.K. also if a strict constructionist judge viewed it as precedent."

So where did Giuliani stand? It wasn't clear, and as noted earlier in my chart, Brand Story Status Concerns, a brand whose positioning is *confusing* in the minds of consumers or voters alike is *inconsistent* and in trouble.

A brand should be reflective: an extension of the beliefs and values of its constituency. **A brand makes headway to the extent it ties into and mirrors the deeply-held beliefs of people and avoids what isn't credible or relevant.** In business, for example, easily the best approach is to sell people on themselves, meaning what they have already internalized and accepted.

In Giuliani's case, by stressing electability he sought to have Republicans select him rationally, making a conscious, calculated choice. He didn't seek personal loyalty. Instead, he hoped that loyal Republican voters would, in effect, see him as the strongest brand option available to avoid the specter of Clinton's election, and decide to support him accordingly.

Lost in Giuliani's strategic calculations was the reality that established values are crucial. Political success depends on aligning yourself with voters' belief systems, which are supremely emotional matters.

EXCLUSIVE: INTO BATTLE WE GO

Ultimately, it's hard to build a positive case for loyalty on negatives alone. But that fact never prevents politicians from trying. Look at Giuliani's candidacy, which he largely based on fighting "Islamo-fascism," saying, "we're going to be in this war for quite some time." The underlying equation had everything to do with first stoking anxiety and then selling himself as the one who could diffuse it.

If McCain's brand story was rooted in fighting the communists in Asia long ago, Giuliani could do him one better. His more up to date story was rooted in resisting Arab fundamentalists who had come to our shores.

The biggest problem with that brand strategy, however, was that in emotional terms Giuliani wasn't selling himself so much as he was fear of others. In short, he wasn't a candidate speaking to an exclusive *we* (he had no base) so much as against a *they*. (Moreover, the fear card wasn't even his to play. It belonged to Bush, who had played it mercilessly for over half a decade by then.)

Edwards tried for us/them brand positioning, too, but to no greater effect. *I've spent my career fighting for underdogs against the powerful special interests*, he earnestly said time and again.

His problem was that he just simply didn't look the part. He didn't appear to belong with the very "us" he was seeking to energize. Derided as the Breck Girl by Rush Limbaugh, Edwards looked preternaturally youthful, with perfect teeth, a smooth, affable style and an upscale lifestyle.

So it fell to Huckabee and to somebody who wasn't even running for president to do us/them branding best. In Huckabee's case he truly looked working class, and that lent credibility to his complains that big CEO salaries are "immoral."

The other us/them player was Ted Kennedy. Apparently, he'd been fuming for months over the way Clinton had picked up and begun to use a line she heard in an introduction for her at a rally in Dover, New Hampshire. There, Francine Torge had introduced the New York senator by saying, "Some people compare one of the other candidates to John F. Kennedy. But he was assassinated. And Lyndon Baines Johnson was the one who actually signed the civil rights bill into law."[19]

But it was the Clintons' attempt to stink-bomb the Obama brand during the South Carolina primary that finally proved to be too much for Kennedy. The result was his endorsement speech of Obama—an instant classic of us/them branding.

Here's how. While the focus of aspirational branding is a dream, the focus of us/them branding is a villain. And Kennedy had one, he felt, in what was really a thinly-veiled, personal rebuttal of Bill and Hillary Clinton's tactics. It is the high road versus the low road. Inspiration versus calculation. The future versus the past. Making those contrasts,

Kennedy spoke with conviction. "With Barrack Obama, we will turn the page on the old politics of misrepresentation and distortion," he roared, and the crowd cheered.

Think of it as blowback. Torge started it unwittingly in Dover with her do-ers versus dreamers' dichotomy. Kennedy paid her back, with interest. He established the dreamers as do-ers with hearts full of integrity. **Great brands are never so broad that there's no "us" and no "them" because to represent all people is impossible and, therefore, meaningless**. What Kennedy did, in effect, was to define the "them" as manipulative cynics the vast majority of people would feel honored *not* to identify with.

GENDER-SENSITIVE: CHANNELING ELEANOR ROOSEVELT

"Iron my shirt!" yelled a man in Salem, New Hampshire, reminding Clinton—as if she needed to be—that misogyny still festers. Almost every brand fights a similar battle. Conscious or unthinking, sexism remains so much of a problem that 91% of women surveyed believe that, based on advertising, companies don't understand them. Meanwhile, 58% of women are deeply annoyed by portrayals of their gender.[20]

Is it any wonder then that Clinton felt like she would have to battle sexism in striving to secure her party's nomination? But ironically, in some ways, Obama exhibited more of the tendencies we traditionally ascribe to women: less combative than Clinton, he also carefully amassed delegates everywhere, cultivating the caucuses to which she paid less attention.

Yes, the Clinton campaign handed out "I can be president" buttons to young girls attending her rallies. Yes, she enjoyed throwing "What does Hillary [women] want?" into her unwavering "concession" speech the night Obama clinched the nomination. Yes, she began her campaign as a "conversation." But by late spring, she was swilling beer and Royal chasers, campaigning from the bed of pickup, and getting praised for her "testicular fortitude" at an Indiana labor rally. Perhaps most notable of all was getting introduced by North Carolina governor Mike Easley as somebody who makes "Rocky Balboa look like a pansy."[21]

What would former first lady Eleanor Roosevelt have made of this? I don't know. But maybe Clinton claims to know. In his latest book, *A Woman in Charge*, Carl Bernstein reports that Clinton once welcomed into the White House a pair of occultists to channel her into Roosevelt's soul.

This much *is* certain. Great brands may tilt either masculine or feminine in their sensibility, reflective of their offer and core audience. But it's smart to build on-emotion brands, ones that won't preclude acceptance by either gender. **Don't adopt a brand strategy that will unintentionally offend or alienate an entire block of people, notably women, who at 54% of the populace are hardly peripheral**.

Clinton clearly assumed she could count on female voters to support her and, Iowa aside that largely proved to be true. But an extra few percentage points of that support early on might have been enough to prevent an Obama breakthrough. If only establishing an easy-going, intimate rapport with her core supporters in meetings held in living rooms had proved as easy as adding a "Likeabiity Tour" of Iowa to her itinerary.

ADAPTIVE: FADE TO BLACK (AND WHITE)

Obama launched his campaign as a man with a mission. In his by now famous words, he didn't see America composed of "red and blue states." He saw the United States of America instead. But over the course of the primary season battle with Clinton, other divisions would emerge. Instead of red and blue melting into a harmonious purple, there would be outbreaks of the old identity politics of African-Americans versus whites, upper class versus working class, as well as urban versus small town.

The net result was a challenge to achieving the goal of the Obama brand and any other emerging brand. That's to reinforce people emotionally, rather than make mistakes that challenge their self-identity and pride.

Here's the arc of what happened to Obama's brand during the primary season, starting with his racial identity. Half-white, half-black, Obama could have easily found himself suffering Giuliani's predicament: a straddler occupying the squishy middle, in the end satisfying no one. How to overcome that fate was Obama's initial hurdle, and he did it well by making moderation seem elevated by promising an era of post-partisan politics.

In doing that, Obama was aided by the on-emotion instincts of being, in the words of Stanford professor Shelby Steele, a natural "bargainer" rather than a "challenger." That is to say, his instinct is to seek out accommodation and compromise—to assume that goodwill will beget goodwill—rather than challenge white society to "make good" on previous injustices.[22] It's a classic divide. Think of Martin Luther King, Jr. versus Malcolm X; Sidney Poitier versus Chris Rock; Michael Jordan versus Dennis Rodman; and, once the internet videos gained notoriety, Obama versus his long-time pastor, the Reverend Jeremiah Wright.

Now, to imagine we live in a color-blind society would be to overlook my company's study of bias, with results in the 40% range regarding the prospect of an African-American president. It would also mean overlooking how Clinton was able to slow Obama's momentum in part by making appeals to, in her own words, "working, hard-working, white Americans."

All things being equal, people prefer comfort. Companies make a lot of money by addressing that desire, and comfort can involve pulling back most naturally to one's own race, one's own tribe, be it African-American, white, or otherwise. That's reality, and Obama would have to deal with it.

Fortunately for the Obama brand, there were three factors favoring him during the primary season, and now beyond it. The first is demographic. The age range of American society is changing. By 2010, Millenials will outnumber Baby-boomers.[23] America's racial composition is also changing, and 40% of Americans will be non-white by 2010.[24]

That diversity, as embodied by the multi-racial Tiger Woods, means the trends favor Obama. He speaks to, and embodies, a changing America.

The second and third factors are particular to Obama. The second is that by manner and facial expressions, Obama is no challenger. Bill Clinton's comparison of Obama to Jesse Jackson couldn't work, in part, because as even an amateur facial coder can readily detect, Obama is a serene politician; in contrast, Jackson, although a disciple of King, has more edge.

The third factor is that comments like "God damn America" weren't said by Obama, but by Wright. Plausible deniability existed as to whether Obama bore witness to Wright's views, even if Obama had been attending Wright's church for years.

So Obama could slide through the first and even the second controversy over Wright's comments—first on video, then at the National Press Club—relatively unscathed. What wasn't so easily maneuvered, however, was Obama's own words at a closed-door fundraiser in San Francisco.

Here is the key statement Obama made about small-town and rural voters: "And it's not surprising then they get bitter, they cling to guns or religion or antipathy to people who aren't like them or anti-immigrant sentiment or anti-trade sentiment as a way to explain their frustrations." Soon thereafter, Obama would claim his remarks were "clumsy" and didn't reflect his true beliefs.[25]

Here, it would be hard to believe him, however.

For one thing, consider where he's lived: Honolulu, Jakarta, Los Angeles, New York, Boston, Chicago, and Washington, D.C. There isn't anything even approaching a small town in the lot. Then as I said in the previous chapter, there's Obama's body language to consider. Sometimes it's haughty and aloof. Moreover, there's finally Obama's entire nature. Sometimes he's the innocent pilgrim, on his way to achieving his own redemption and the country's at the same time. At other times, however, he's more the prince: dignified, regal, and detached .

In the end, just as Giuliani has a dual personality—that of the Broadway Priest—so is Obama's identity a blend that leads me to think of him as the Pilgrim Prince. Is there an air of elitism to him? Absolutely. He might say his anthropologist mom had lived on food stamps. But she also took care, and found a way, to send him to one of the finest secondary schools Hawaii had to offer.[26]

So there was, and is, a large potential gap between Obama and largely white, rural and small-town voters about whom he spoke in San Francisco. It was a gap Clinton recognized, and a campaign opportunity to which she adapted. What she said well after Obama's fundraiser remarks became known was that "Senator Obama's remarks are elitist and out of touch. They are not reflective of the values and beliefs of Americans... People don't need a president who looks down on them. They need a president who stands up for them."

Now, Clinton (Wellesley '69, Yale Law '73) was hardly the second coming of Norma Rae. It didn't matter. Branding doesn't work that way. The point is that the people Clinton was speaking to *wanted* to believe her, and that's enough. Obama had harmed his candidacy by enabling his rival to build a brand that made at least a certain segment of voters feel more comfortable, happy, proud and successful by identifying with her brand, than his.

You want to build a brand that reinforces pride, instead of being an obstacle to it. Most of all, **you never want to be the enemy of your target audience's belief systems**. Yes, Obama tried to make amends. To enable his brand to stay on-emotion, he knew he needed to reinvest in his emotional relationship with the voters he dismissively referred to in San Francisco. But to that end, going out and bowling a ludicrous score of 37 wasn't and won't be enough.

CONCLUSION

Being on-emotion in branding terms requires, first and foremost, transcending the offer. It requires an emotional connection with people that ultimately rests more on faith than functionality alone. Romney never got that, but Obama did. His candidacy is in large part a testimony to the power of branding. He's consciously written his life's story into the fabric of the country's imagination by tying it to larger stories: Lincoln's, and the 1960s legacy of the Kennedys and Martin Luther King, Jr. At the same time, however, he's sought to avoid the acrimony of that era.

As Edwards and Giuliani learned, branding works best when the "us" reverberates with more emotional strength and validity than the depiction of the other party, the "them." In essence, branding is about spurring a desire to belong to a brand whose values, imagery and associations compel you. For example, by calling himself a Main-Street as opposed to a Wall-Street type Republican and "Authentic Conservative," Huckabee opted for positioning himself as both down-to-earth and real.

4 COMMUNICATIONS

Candidate as Advertised

OVERVIEW

Some Republicans have complained that McCain is essentially a candidate without an ideology. But if McCain's reverence for Teddy Roosevelt as his favorite presidential role model is any indication, he does have a mold he fits into: that of moderate, reform-minded politician.[1]

To date, McCain has applied his reformer instincts mostly notably to campaign finance reform. But in 2004, that instinct carried over into advertising. During that campaign, his reaction to the Swift Boat commercials attacking Kerry's military record was to call the people who created them lacking in "decency." In McCain's words, these were people who "should hang their heads in shame" for doubting Kerry's bravery in Vietnam.[2]

Sensory Logic has used facial coding over the past decade to test corporate advertising. Political ads, however, have their own special challenges, including smaller budgets and tighter timelines. In the starkly combative political realm—where the fight between candidates takes on personal overtones—factoring in where to draw the line in terms of negative advertising also needs to be made.

That last question, in particular, involves an on-emotion judgment. Is an attack ad effective? Does it taint its sponsoring candidate by striking voters as simply "too much"? Perhaps the blows don't actually land at all, generating little if any emotional reaction from voters. This chapter is devoted in part to answering those very questions.

The material here is broader than just advertising. Stump speeches and the role of the internet, particularly in regard to viral video and the candidates' web sites, will also be discussed. The overall focus is on the goals any version of communications must realize. On a strategic level, they consist of being **hopeful**, **values-driven**, **relevant**, **believable**, and **reassuring**. Tactically, success comes from being **visually-driven**, **understandable**, **memorable**, **dynamic**, and **personalized**. (For a full description of each of these goals, see Appendix C.)

Soon I will show how different forms of communication during the campaign season have illuminated each of those goals. But first let's set the stage by seeing how a very famous political TV spot performed when my company tested it using facial coding.

THE RESULTS FROM FACIALLY CODING RESPONSES TO "DAISY"

Lyndon Baines Johnson's 1964 TV spot, "Daisy," aired only once but is still widely considered to be the greatest piece of political campaign advertising ever. It opens with a young girl picking the petals off a flower. Suddenly, an ominous voice begins a countdown that ends with an image of a mushroom cloud from a nuclear bomb explosion, followed by a warning not to vote for Barry Goldwater because his views are so extreme he might take America into a nuclear war.

To provide readers with a context in which to compare our facially coded assessments of how the 2008 political commercials performed, my company tested "Daisy." Here's what we found.

LBJ's "Daisy": Strikingly On-Emotion

As my analysis will explain more fully, LBJ's ad is absolutely a home run. The little girl's presence on screen is supposed to lift voters' hearts. It does: appeal is high. Then the threat to the little girl—and to all of us—creates an on-emotion collapse of the appeal score. The final rise in appeal is when LBJ offers himself as the solution to avoid a catastrophe.

In simplest terms, there are three key ways in which to read these or any facially coded second-by-second results. First, what's the *volume* of emotional data points? In other words, how often did voters have an emotional response?

These data points are calculated based on having multiple voters respond to the TV spot at exactly the same split-second. (There are other single, "stray cat" reactions happening throughout the commercial; however, they don't get shown on the chart because they lack critical mass.) A good TV spot will have at least ten to twelve of these emotional data points. "Daisy" has thirteen, spread nicely throughout so that no stretch of the TV spot has an emotional "bald spot."

Secondly, what are the impact (intensity) and appeal (likeability) *levels*? Third, how good is the *fit*? Is the commercial on-emotion? Do the impact and appeal levels—and the feelings they're based on—fit the execution, appropriate to what's happening on screen and what the candidacy's strategy is seeking to achieve? In these two ways, "Daisy" excels. Notice the huge, compelling—entirely on-emotion—high/low swing in appeal as this spot goes from the charming little girl, counting the petals on a daisy, to a countdown leading to an atomic explosion.

Now, let's see how well the top ten on-emotion goals of great communications were put into action on the campaign trail.

BELIEVABLE: CAN'T AFFORD A FOOL

By nature, McCain doesn't play it light. Terse and tight, frozen smiles, and clenched teeth pretty well describes McCain's body language. As he speaks, either his index finger or his entire hand often points down, repeatedly thrusting. In short, McCain is a snake stomper: an often angry man known to draw black-and-white distinctions, such as calling other politicians "stupid" and worse.[3]

A stranger to excessive hope, McCain's talk is peppered with phrases like, "There are no easy answers, my friends" and "These are dangerous and serious times." Back in high school, McCain's friends nicknamed him "McNasty" due to his temper. Now he's a man who describes himself as "old as dirt, with more scars than Frankenstein." As to his favorite animals, he admits to liking rats "because they're cunning and they eat well."[4]

Clearly not saccharine, McCain doesn't favor creating soft, sweet TV spots, either. In Romney, he had a rival he could relish defeating—and, of course, did, as our facial coding of voters' response to an anti-Romney spot predicted.

Romney is sort of an anti-Horatio Alger story who was born wealthy and today is even wealthier. But McCain couldn't really begrudge Romney his fortune, being married as he is to the daughter of a man who created one of the country's most lucrative Budweiser distributorships. The difference between them rests more in a clash of temperaments. Romney's *Leave It to Beaver* tendency is to say "gosh" and "my goodness." McCain's is to skirmish and swear at others, including his Republican colleagues.[5]

Posted on McCain's web site just days before the New Hampshire primary, the new TV spot alerted undecided voters (and the media) to a weakness in Romney that McCain hoped might derail his rival. What did McCain's anti-Romney "Issue Alert" spot consist of? On screen, voters see Romney's image and the words "[a] president doesn't need foreign policy experience," which the voice-over repeats. That point of attack created the first, negative-appeal data point captured in our testing.

"Issue Alert": McCain Knocking Romney Down

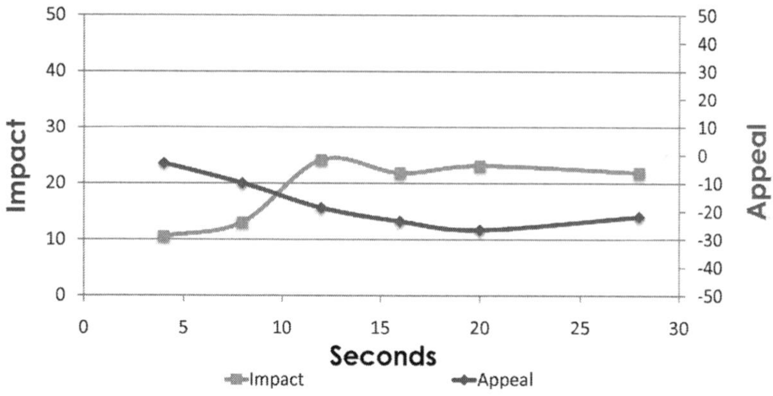

In "Issue Alert," McCain successfully attaches negative emotions to Romney. Appeal dips as the narrator recalls quotes from Romney that might strike voters as foolish. Images of Romney are juxtaposed with images of the danger America may face.

Then viewers see Romney on screen saying that if America needs a leader with foreign policy experience, "we can simply go to the State Department." That statement is followed by an image of gun-toting Islamic fighters, which lowers the appeal score even more.

All of that, however, is just the set-up for the climatic one-two punch, which lands squarely. First, McCain challenges Romney: "Is he serious?" That's followed by, "We live in a dangerous world and these are serious times." Voters' emotional response to this sequence caused the appeal score to hit its lowest point.

Was it an effective TV spot? Absolutely, as it successfully labels Romney as naive for failing to recognize the extent of America's need for a leader with foreign policy experience. As in LBJ's "Daisy" spot, the strategy was to paint an opponent as too risky for the American public to choose as president. McCain's spot did well by driving the appeal score repeatedly downward the longer Romney's face appeared on screen.

Unlike LBJ's spot, however, McCain didn't benefit from the implied comparison with his rival. During the close of "Daisy," invoking LBJ's name lifts the appeal score by 20 points. In contrast, introducing McCain on screen in this spot provides no more than a five point lift in appeal. "Issue Alert" also isn't as engaging as "Daisy," amassing only half as many emotional data points (six versus 13).

Nevertheless, McCain's spot achieved its basic objective—labeling Romney as foolish. And it sticks with that agenda, which is harder than it might sound. That's because finding a central theme and staying conceptually clean and simple is difficult. For instance, my company also tested a Romney TV spot that opens by labeling him a winner. Voters' positive response led to a high appeal score. But as the TV spot moved on to a barrage of video clips of Romney, a bald spot emerged—no emotional response—as the viewing voters felt overwhelmed and gave up.

The point here is that McCain's negative thrust works because it does what all great advertising accomplishes. **It attaches one fantastically appropriate adjective, and one easily understood benefit to the offer and, in doing so, helps distinguish that offer from those of rivals**. Romney the *fool* versus McCain the *hero* is enough here.

Moreover, that's true because Romney's campaign was premised on his being a *smart*, capable businessman. The savvy strategy is to take a rival's strength and find a weakness in it, and do so in a way that gives the public a single, striking reason to care. McCain's spot did that.

The central human truth of this category, foreign affairs, is to keep Americans safe (and free of fear), which McCain promised to do. Meanwhile, Romney's TV spot, with its talk of strengthening the military, was effectively undercut. A fool who doesn't know how to use a strong military because of naivete about foreign affairs is of no value. McCain capitalized on that and received the advantage.

HOPEFUL: DUSK IN AMERICA

Running for re-election in 1984, Reagan released his upbeat, cheerful TV spot, "Morning in America." In 2008, the entire field of Republican candidates tried to emulate the confidence and success of Reagan in debates and speeches. But when we tested their primary season commercials with voters, we found that those felt more like dusk in America instead.

In comparison to the Democratic candidates' TV spots that we also tested, the Republicans were burdened with a problem I'll call the "hope gap." Because hope sells, a failure to embody and project optimism is usually the equivalent of electoral suicide.

One way to quantify the Republicans' hope gap is to look at the second-by-second results. We tested 14 Republican spots and 15 Democratic spots. The Republicans netted 114 emotional data points versus the Democrats' 129 data points, indicating that the Democrats were more successful in sparking voters' interest. In regard to the hope gap, only seven (of 114) Republican data points reached the threshold of a solid positive appeal score, a measly 6%. For the Democrats, the ratio was 29 (of 129) or 20%, a 14% advantage over the Republicans.

Further evidence of the hope gap is that the highest, positive appeal point for the Republicans came, regrettably enough, in reaction to a spiteful comment. At second four of the Tancredo TV spot we tested, the appeal shoots upward as Tancredo declares that "more than 15 million illegal aliens have invaded our land." Obviously, the message itself was not positive. But Tancredo's aggressive anti-immigrant phrasing suggested that, if elected, he would take action to solve the problem, thereby inspiring the lift in appeal.

As for how the Democrats inspired their highest positive appeal points, the story is much different. No candidate was able to equal voters' highly positive reception to the opening of a Richardson TV spot. In it, the narrator begins by heralding "The New Mexico comeback—a model for the nation," which credits the state's economic growth to Richardson's effective governance. That very upbeat opening was positively on-emotion, netting four high appeal points within the spot's first five seconds.

Only one other single emotional data point equaled Richardson's robust opening, which was the reaction to Obama's tagline: "Change you can believe in." Appearing in a TV spot otherwise devoted to soberly talking about the need to reduce America's dependence on foreign oil, the tagline's hopeful promise clearly lifted voters' hearts.

Finally, one other way to quantify the Republicans hope gap is to look at the overall impact and appeal scores for the candidates' individual TV spots, as plotted on a quadrant chart. Compare the respective charts for the two parties. What you'll quickly see is that the Democrats had five TV spots in or near positive appeal territory, while the Republicans had none.

Results for Democratic TV Spots

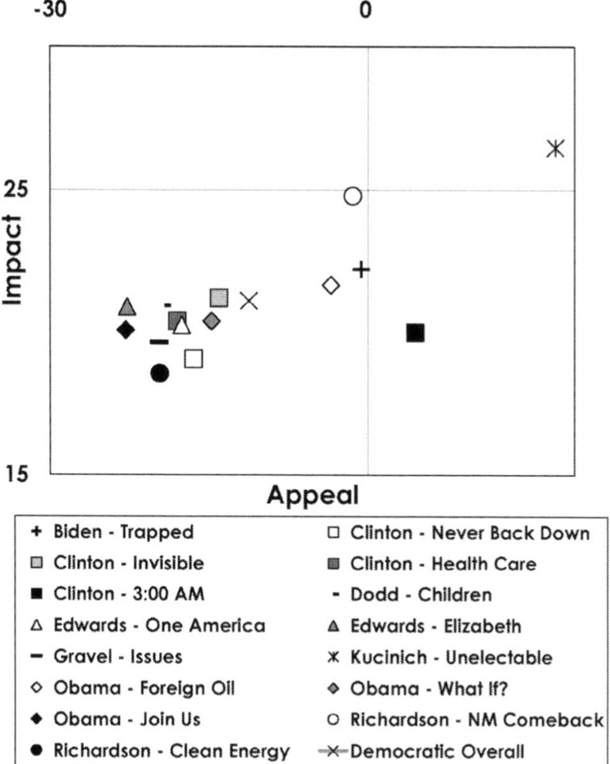

Most of the candidates' TV spots struggled to create a happy, positive response in the party faithful. Kucinich did, but given the content voters might have been laughing at him as often as with him. Clinton, Obama, Biden and Richardson each created one spot otherwise best able to sell hope.

Results for Republican TV Spots

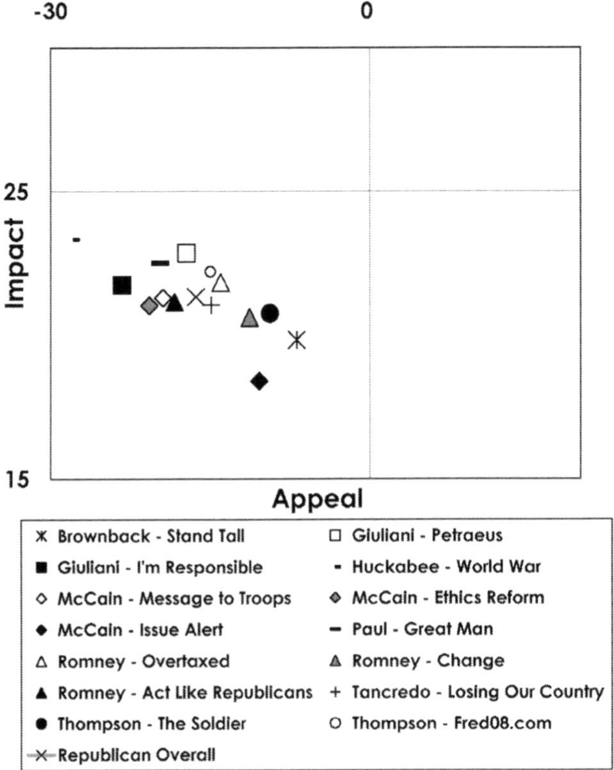

Unwilling or unable to sell hope, the Republican candidates released TV spots that echoed Reagan's complaint about the "doom-and-gloom" Democrats of old. Hamstrung by poor funding, even the early Huckabee spot we tested failed to convey his usual cheer.

Far ahead of anybody else in appeal is Kucinich, with a zany commercial, which is a hit-and-miss affair. Kucinich scored high numbers as he makes fun of his short physical stature ("You really cut those guys down to size in those debates"). However, in making light of his lack of electability ("I am electable, if you vote for me!") he drew a weak response.

Despite Kucinich's ultimate failure as a candidate, let me reiterate that inspiring happiness and hope matters. One of the country's leading psychologists, Martin Seligman, has studied voters' response to a candidate's level of optimism based on the wording of their speeches. Analyzing the speeches given by presidential candidates in races between 1900 and 1988, he found that optimism sells.

In fact, in 19 of 23 of those contests as coded for optimism by Seligman, the more optimistic candidate won. That's an 82.6% correlation. Moreover, Seligman's study found that the greater the margin of optimism in a candidate versus his opponent, the greater the margin of the general election victory.[6]

In summary, in presidential races people favor optimism, just as they do in daily life. As demonstrated by Obama's well-received tagline, creating hope and the prospect of a positive net outcome works. **Great advertising always address the human desire for something big, new and positive.** Show people how you will enhance or protect their lives, and they will reward you by giving their support.

RELEVANT: LONGING TO ESCAPE

In *The Wizard of Oz*, Judy Garland sings "Somewhere Over The Rainbow," expressing the universal longing to transcend current limitations and experience a life of endless joy. In 2008, that longing to escape often took very specific, partisan shape. For the Democrats, a desire for America to exit the fighting in Iraq was front and center. Among Republicans, taxation remained an issue that guaranteed an emotional reaction.

Let's start with the Democrats first, and a TV spot by Biden critiquing the situation in Iraq. Aside from a good government spot by Obama and a clean energy spot by Richardson, no other commercial created by a Democratic candidate was so clearly relevant and resulted in as many second-by-second emotional data points as Biden's. And that's despite its fatal flaw.

Trapped by Irrelevancy

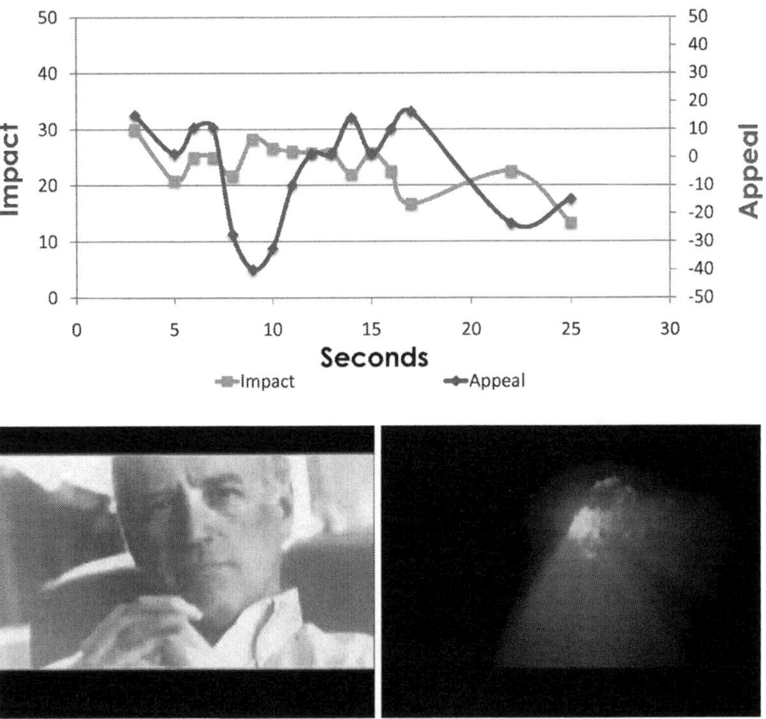

In "Trapped," Biden compares America's situation in Iraq to being trapped in a hole. What's worse than that (for a politician)? The emotional indifference voters showed when Biden came on screen as the solution to America's troubles.

Certainly, the opening is emotionally effective. Among the voters we tested, 14 of the first 17 seconds evoke a reaction. A provocative visual metaphor provides the explanation. Biden's spot opens with video shot from the perspective of a person trapped below ground, looking up out of a hole at a small patch of sunlight overhead. "Imagine you're trapped deep in a hole," the narrator begins, making the horror all the worse by adding: "with a group of politicians."

On-cue and on-emotion, the high appeal score occasioned by the spot's opening jab at politicians then takes a huge dip. Why? That's because the narrator has gone on to add, "President Bush says the only way out of Iraq is to dig us deeper and deeper."

Talk about being on-emotion: among the seven core emotions facial coding can gauge, 16% of the emotional response to this spot involves anxiety, a total exceeded only by the 19% McCain was able to generate while attacking Romney's lack of foreign policy experience. Where does that anxiety become prevalent? The answer is that voters feel their greatest degree of anxiety on hearing that Bush is apparently in favor of digging America into an ever deeper hole in Iraq.

On-emotion yet again, the appeal score then recovers, lifts, and hits a pair of high points as viewers are promised, "We can get out now without leaving chaos behind."

So far, so good—for the Biden campaign. Disaster, however, is just around the corner. Right after second 17, the small patch of sunlight that had turned into an entire screen of hazy sunshine, gets transformed. An image of Biden himself now emerges, as if from heaven. He is hardly considered an archangel, as far as viewers are apparently concerned. Only a pair of emotional data points appear in response to the remainder of this spot. One is when the narrator states that Biden alone has "a plan to end this war responsibly." The other is in reaction to the phrase, "so our children don't have to go back."

Otherwise, from the moment Biden's image comes on screen, the emotional data points stop. By the numbers, before Biden's face is shown on screen, 82% of the commercial spurs an emotional response. When Biden is present, the percentage drops to 15%. In other words, is the Iraq war seen as a highly relevant issue? Absolutely. Was Biden seen as highly relevant in terms of providing a solution? No.

The bottom line here is that Biden could tout his foreign policy credentials all he wanted, but voters weren't buying. Age was surely part of the explanation. "Forty four Senators are older than me," I heard Biden say in one of his stump speeches—a fact that could leave listeners concerned about the retirement home known as Capitol Hill. Among the voters we interviewed, one quote best reflects this facial coding data. Biden was seen as an "old-style politician" who "doesn't represent anything new."

While the Iraq war was haunting the Democratic candidates, taxation obviously remains an eternal, evergreen issue among Republicans. Both Paul and Romney addressed it, getting a strong emotional response from voters. Paul's spot, stressing liberty—and freedom from the IRS—garnered the second most emotional data points among the Republican spots we tested. Romney's attack on the "death tax" came in fifth.

How on-emotion was Romney's spot? Good enough that his punning statement, let's "Kill the death tax," enjoyed a spike in appeal as did his promising a "new tax rate." In contrast, as a long roll call of the taxes currently being paid by Americans scrolled across the screen, the appeal score dipped in response.

But as effective as it was, Romney's spot couldn't match Paul's passionate delivery on the subject of taxes. Among Republicans, only Giuliani, speaking of fiscal responsibility, also managed a string of five emotional data points in a row, second by second. How did Paul manage to do so? By clearly, emphatically saying his opposition to taxes was rooted in the principle of never having "to sacrifice one bit of liberty."

In that TV spot by Paul, as well as a speech excerpt of his, which we also facially coded voters' response to, the taxation versus liberty theme repeatedly created an emotional response. It's not hard to see why. **Great advertising depends on establishing relevancy.** The desire to *defend* a resource, like money, is one of the Four Core Motivations, as established by Harvard University psychologists Lawrence and Nohria.[7] The desires to *acquire, learn, and bond with others* round out the list.

Relevancy brings both votes and buyers. Paul was able to inspire twice as much of an emotional response as Romney to the very same issue. Why? Romney approached it more rationally. In contrast, Paul framed the issue broadly and deeply, as a matter of liberty and emotionally-driven values. He inspired a response by turning a desire to escape taxation into a fundamental human right and need.

MEMORABLE: THE APPLE OF YOUR EYE

From the first time I met him, I knew Paul was an original. At the Ames Straw Poll, I was at Paul's tent when I saw him choose not to kiss a baby presented to him but, rather, autograph the baby's diaper instead. Such spontaneity and unorthodoxy was shown in more profound ways, too. For instance, Paul proved to be the only candidate in either party who decided to reveal, and in real-time, the dollars and the names of donors as they rolled in.[8]

By doing so, Paul transformed his website. His Republican rivals, as well as Clinton, settled for treating their websites primarily as a donation vehicle and free TV station for their videos. But in Paul's case, his website became an authentic, principles-in-action ad for his candidacy, to a degree matched only by Obama's website.

Obama and Paul alone embraced the grassroots, bottoms-up mentality of the internet—and were, in turn, embraced by a flood of supporters. The numbers are truly staggering. Using the plan-your-own gatherings, "meet-ups" strategy first developed by the Howard Dean campaign in 2004, the Paul team allowed loyalists to all but take over his campaign. Before long, supporters had arranged for over 1,000 spontaneous campaign gatherings, involving over 900 cities, and in excess of 65,000 members.[9]

Meanwhile, Obama's numbers were, if anything, even more impressive. Before he began amassing a string of victories in February of 2008, Obama was already winning in other ways. By then his Facebook page was already linked to more than 500,000 supporters (five times the number Clinton had, and eight times more than McCain)[10]. His videos had also by then already been viewed nearly 18 million times, triple Clinton's total and nine times McCain's total.[11]

In contrast, other campaigns faced difficulties with their use of the internet. In the beginning of 2008, for instance, McCain's Facebook profile link didn't work, Huckabee was without a video library, and much of Edwards' site hadn't been updated since May 2007.[12] But nobody would prove to be less adept in this new medium than Clinton.

The problem wasn't so much what Clinton was doing or failing to do with her site. Yes, photos her team posted to the website frequently neglected to name the people in them. Yes, letters or messages from Clinton came with an obviously pasted-in copy of her signature. Yes, the videos on the site weren't as real as those on other websites. For example, clips of her speeches, as shown on TV, were recycled, as opposed to the videos the Obama team took of their crowds of supporters.[13]

On a tactical level, all those mishaps were merely errors. On a broader brand level, however, each of these communications missteps fed into a more threatening problem: an image of Clinton as nothing less than a distant, cold, self-righteous, judgmental, calculating professional politician. As such, she helped set herself up as the perfect foil for the "Vote Different" ("1984") video spoof that as of July 2008 had received over five million views.[14]

Images from "Vote Different"

This anti-Clinton video was anonymously created. Its title is a rallying cry that deliberately echoes Apple's long-running "Think Different" campaign. Endorsing individuality, it depicts Clinton as authoritarian; Big Brother has become Big Sister.

"Vote Different" is a spoof of the famous "1984" commercial by Apple (Computer). In that case, the target was Big Blue (IBM), implicitly compared to the Big Brother government portrayed in George Orwell's nightmarish *1984* novel about a future totalitarian state. But in 2008, Clinton, not IBM, had now become the target.

Again, as in the Apple spot, the people on screen consist of jackbooted police and the worker drones they control, transfixed by a large screen on which their leader is talking. This time it's Clinton, with excerpts from her own speeches and announcements. Among the excerpts are, "I don't want people who already agree with me" and "we all need to be part of the discussion if we're all going to be part of the solution."

In effect, the spoof demonstrates just how off-emotion Clinton's communications efforts were. Sustained loyalty depends on creating feelings of likeability and trust in supporters. Later in the campaign, Clinton's public appearances would be described more positively by reporters on the campaign trail. But initially, the reviews described her as lacking the ability to connect with people, reinforcing the "Vote Different" video's critique.

"Be part of our team," rolls across the big, icy blue-gray screen in the video. "This is our conversation," rolls, too, undercutting Clinton's emotional brand equity. What brings this incredibly well executed critique to an end? It's a female athlete who, wearing the Obama sunrise symbol on her top, hurls a sledgehammer into the screen, causing it to explode.

The video's final image is the Apple logo, shown in a rainbow of colors. That fits because many of the Obama videos atop the list of most-viewed videos have the flavor of the Apple commercials on TV. Obama's candidate-generated videos show a mostly young, racially diverse group of people. They're enjoying themselves as they proclaim their support of Obama. Striving to be both authentic and on-emotion in portraying hope, those videos feel very natural, the opposite of how Clinton is depicted in the "1984" spoof.

Speaking of Apple, when asked by *Politico* if he was a PC or a Mac supporter, McCain admitted he was "Neither. I am an illiterate who has to rely on my wife for all of the assistance that I can get."[15] Clearly, the internet is a phenomenon largely passing McCain by. Look at this list of the top 10 most-viewed, politically-oriented videos on YouTube.[16] What's striking? Like the Beatles in 1964, the top of the chart is dominated by Obama. Both the lone pro-Clinton and pro-McCain videos barely qualify for the list, comparatively speaking.

Top Ten YouTube Political Videos

Candidate	Title	Views	Released
Pro-Obama	**Yes We Can**	**8,564,449**	**2-Feb-08**
Anti-Clinton	Vote Different	5,292,286	5-Mar-07
Pro-Obama	**A More Perfect Union**	**4,621,348**	**18-Mar-08**
Pro-Obama	**Empire Strikes Barack**	**1,557,731**	**1-May-08**
Pro-Obama	**Response to State of the Union**	**1,416,683**	**28-Jan-08**
Pro-Obama	**Iowa Victory Speech**	**1,286,488**	**3-Jan-08**
Anti-Clinton	Beat the Bitch	1,211,953	13-Nov-07
Anti-Clinton	Coffee Machine Gaffe	975,420	30-Apr-08
Pro-Clinton	I Need Your Advice	656,171	16-May-07
Pro-McCain	Bill Clinton on McCain	390,952	7-Dec-07

In the end, it could be argued convincingly that the real originality of "advertising" circa the 2008 race no longer exists in traditional media. Except for Biden's Iraq TV spot, Kucinich's odd interview of himself, and perhaps one or two instances, none of the spots the candidates have distributed have been notably creative or memorable. Lots of U.S. flags waving in the background and the candidate speaking to the camera doesn't cut through very well anymore.

Today we have a battle between citizen-generated content versus the candidates' attempt to control their messages. Which one feels more on-emotion and authentic is clear. **The weakness of top-down message delivery versus the power of social networking lies in the latter's independent spirit, which helps to make the communication efforts more real, hotter, and thus more likely to inspire recall.** Nothing illustrates that axiom like the "Vote Different" video, with its accurate prediction: "You'll see. 2008 won't be like '1984'." Yes, Obama took Clinton down. It's a game of rock, paper, scissors. In terms of effectiveness, word-of-mouth-endorsements beat broadcast advertising, but is now beaten, in turn, by memorable on-line video.

REASSURING: THE VENGEFUL COOK

Before Clinton, Edwards and Obama gave their respective speeches at the Democrats' Jefferson-Jackson Dinner in Iowa in November 2007, Rove had Obama at 20-to-one odds to win the nomination. Afterwards, he dropped the odds to five-to-one. What did Rove hear that changed his mind?

Two words provide the answer: separation and repetition. The first word, separation, comes from Obama's favorite sport: basketball. It refers to trying to create enough space between yourself and the person guarding you that you can get your shot off without risk of it being blocked. Separation is what Obama alone among the three major Democratic candidates achieved at the Jefferson-Jackson Dinner, as I will soon explain.

What did Clinton do there? She didn't go for separation but, rather repetition. Repetition suited her because it's a traditional tool of political rhetoric, setting up the audience to expect a line or phrase that turns into a chant.

Here's what Clinton repeated. There were 15 variations of promising to fight or praising those who fight (like the soldiers in Iraq). Then as set up by Harry Truman's famous remark, "If you can't stand the heat, get out of the kitchen," Clinton segued to "I feel really comfortable in the kitchen." From there, it was but a small step to, "We should be turning up the heat on the Republicans; they deserve all the heat we can give them." In all, the speech would contain a dozen instances when the metaphor would be used, even if it was the audience being encouraged to say the phrase.

The point of Clinton's repetition was to reassure her audience that she was tough enough to be America's first female commander-in-chief. But how smart or necessary was it for her to make that her focus? The voters who rated the candidates for us, earlier in 2007, showed that they already saw Clinton as the strongest, toughest person in the race. In advertising terms, Clinton was, therefore, seeking to own an adjective (like fast, reliable, et cetera) that she already owned.

Clinton Primed to Fight

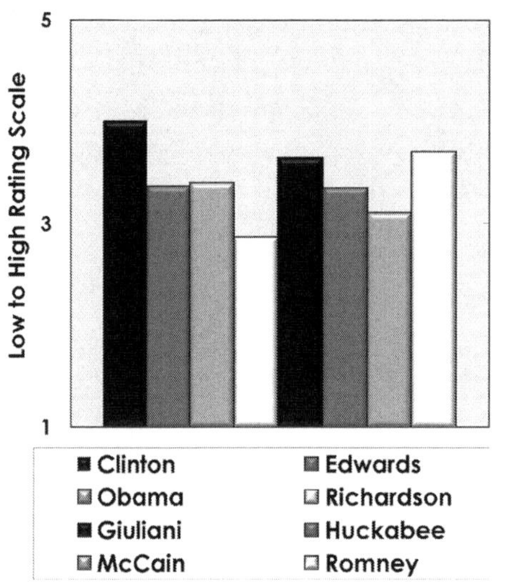

On average, no candidate was seen by voters as exuding more personal strength than Clinton. Through a prolonged primary season battle, she proved the voters' ratings apt.

Fighting does, indeed, fit the Clinton mentality and track record. She was the person who had set up her husband's War Room, voted for the war in Iraq, and favors annihilating Iran if it attacks Israel. But emphasizing a desire to fight also boxed Clinton in. It's hard to be convincingly on-emotion about seeking vengeance and promising generosity both at once. Try as she might, Clinton could not resolve the contradiction just by saying, as she did on winning the New Hampshire primary, "Finding common ground ... has been the cause of my life."[17]

Clinton was not able to co-opt Obama's brand promise in New Hampshire, preserving the separation Obama had achieved in Iowa at the Jefferson-Jackson Dinner. There, Clinton and Edwards alike spoke in terms of fighting the opposition. Obama alone spoke of inviting everyone into his campaign, including Democrats, Republicans and Independents. In this spirit of reconciliation, he created the separation and differentiation his candidacy needed to buck the odds.[18]

In seeking to reassure voters, Clinton forgot that real assurance isn't shrill. **Credibility doesn't get established as a result of the emotional equivalent of shouting**. You can't rush or bully people into giving you their trust. Like every other form of evaluation, finding *value* in someone is an emotional assessment. Someone who would relish the notion of people (Republicans) being, in effect, baked alive, will cause us to doubt that person's humanity. Clinton's repetition was believable, but Obama's separation was likeable.

VALUES-DRIVEN: I'M OKAY, YOU'RE FULL OF IT

Being a divisive or unifying figure is a both a matter of political strategy and a candidate's natural orientation. Taken to their extremes, the two options are difficult if not impossible to reconcile authentically. So it would be understandable if a voter's head might spin on hearing Clinton switch from wanting to give the opposition "heat" to saying instead, "I hope I will never, ever find myself being defensive or abrupt and dismissive of people who disagree with me."[19]

The Republican equivalent to Clinton's inconsistency would be Giuliani and his TV spot, "I'm Responsible." In it he tells his fellow Americans: "It's clear that what unites us is far greater than what divides us." Coming from Giuliani, famous for the degree to which he gleefully mocks his rivals, the statement's sincerity is off-emotion for him, and the voters we tested seemed to feel the same way.

Indeed, voters' anxiety levels spiked just then, an emotional response that might be partly explained by Giuliani's body language. As he makes the statement, he lifts his eyebrows, cocks his head, and changes his tone of voice. The overall affect is theatrical at best, play-acting at worst, thereby undercutting Giuliani's attempt at empathetic sincerity. But besides responding to a dubious messenger and an over-done delivery, voters may have also felt uneasy about the statement because it's dubious, given how polarized American politics has become. To be frank about it, facial coding serves as an excellent *bullshit detector.*

Two candidates whose commercials couldn't survive the scrutiny of facial coding to verify emotional response, or lack thereof, were Romney and Thompson. As I touched on earlier, in Romney's case, we tested voters' response to the "Thank You, Iowa" spot he ran after winning the Ames Straw Poll. Romney's endlessly repeated campaign platform of wanting to strengthen the military, the economy, and the family generated, in this case, only a single emotional data point when uttered, signaling its inability to connect emotionally with voters.

Nor did Thompson's campaign theme of "Security, Unity, Prosperity" fare much better. Actually, it fared even worse. Appearing on screen at the end of his "Fate Depends on Unity" spot, those three thematic words failed to generate any significant emotional response whatsoever.

The inability of Romney and Thompson to resonate with voters through their commercials didn't bode well for their speechmaking efforts, either. I wasn't at all surprised by how they were received at the Family Research Council's Values Voter Summit held in Washington, D.C. in October of 2007. In that case, it wasn't facial coding that would determine the results. It was the religious, fundamentalist community's own instincts telling them who they should and shouldn't believe.

Only three of the Republican candidates had any realistic chance of winning the gathering's straw poll. Of them, I counted out Thompson immediately. He didn't enjoy the advantages of Romney's organizational strength and money or Huckabee's authenticity. In a fight based on passion alone, I figured Huckabee would win. When my company tested excerpts of speeches from every Republican contender, Paul and Huckabee had come in first and second in creating emotional engagement. They came across convincingly, articulating their beliefs and values in ways people could relate to with ease. Meanwhile, Romney had come in second-to-last and Thompson dead last.

How did each of these three candidates' speeches resonate at the Values Voter Summit? As a former businessman, Romney spent a large part of his speech devoted to the family as "the economic unit of our society"—and paid the price. To Romney, "financial resources" meant speaking about wealth in terms of *money*, whereas his audience was really more intent on hearing about a wealth of *faith*. In turn, Thompson wandered off into another history lesson about the Founding Fathers.

That left Huckabee as the emotionally viable option. He alone spoke from the heart regarding his beliefs and lifestyle. While he chose not to mention that the Rolling Stones are his favorite band, nor sing a few lines from "Get Off of My Cloud," he nevertheless managed to have some fun in expressing his values.

Huckabee repeated the following story: *a woman asks him, Are you one of those narrow-minded Baptists who think only Baptists will go to heaven? I said, lady, no. Actually I'm more narrow than that. I don't think all the Baptists are going to make it.* Then he criticized Romney and Thompson, in effect, challenging their authenticity and calling them off-emotion by saying, "There are many who will seek our support. But let me say that it's important that people sing from their hearts and don't merely lip-synch the lyrics to our songs."

Did Huckabee's own on-emotion speech work? Almost. In fact he would have won the straw poll if it had been a fair fight. The Values Voter Summit was the largest gathering of Republicans after the Ames Straw Poll and prior to the national convention in St. Paul. But ballots submitted electronically prior to the event also count. There, Romney's well-funded organizational muscle had enabled him to build such a strong lead that he narrowly won. That's true even though those who heard the candidates speak in person broke in Huckabee's favor by a 40% margin.[20]

Clearly, true passion sells. It's easier to be on-emotion when the feelings are real and genuinely mirror your audience's beliefs and values. Don't try to get people to change their hearts and minds. In politics, as in business or life in general, there's little upside to making the attempt. Instead, **link your message to what people have already internalized and emotionally endorsed** because it's always easier to sell people on themselves.

PERSONALIZED: SPEED KILLS

To create a strong sense of "us"—a sense of being in it together with voters—isn't a facile exercise. It requires real intimacy, real commitment. Otherwise, the "I" that's part of "us" will come off as merely a case of ego and personal ambition. And that's fatal.

Every politician handles the intimacy challenge a little differently, of course. Out of curiosity, I started investigating this challenge by going through the speeches of the major Republican contenders and counting just how often either first person singular or plural pronouns arise in their speeches. I wanted to see just how explicitly they were committing themselves to a relationship with voters. Only a sampling was involved, but there were enough speeches to detect a pattern. Not surprisingly perhaps, the two candidates with the biggest personal brands, McCain and Giuliani, both used "I" most often. In fact, they used it over 20% more than Thompson did and over 30% more than Romney or Huckabee.

Meanwhile, use of the royal "we" varied, too. In McCain's case, it's often been a sort of I/you relationship that he tries to strike with voters, as in "I trust you" [to see it my way]. In Giuliani's case, however, little attempt was made to foster a personal bond with the audience. When it arose, the "we" primarily centered on what a Giuliani administration would accomplish. Finally, to round out the comparison, the other three candidates tended to use "we" in referring either to Americans in general or their supporters in particular.

Switching over to the Democrats, we're going to look at two examples of the value of being intimate and on-emotion. The in-depth analysis involves what I observed by watching Clinton firsthand in New Hampshire. But first let's consider Edwards. Want to know the power of being personal? Consider this result from an Edwards TV spot we tested, called "One America." The results start out well. There are five emotional data points in the first six seconds—indicating lots of interest in the candidate—and a nice rise in the appeal score as Edwards says: "I believe in the politics of what's possible."

The camera is on him, up close. He's speaking slowly, softly. The appeal scores are decent, meaning people like this guy.

Then the voters suddenly cease to be engaged, and here's why. First, Edwards is suddenly shown from afar, on stage, while the other half of the screen is taken up by the words, "The Edward's Plan," and the image of a thick, white paper document. That's already bad enough. After all, the plan is obviously long—therefore complicated and a pain to read.

Edwards Loses Contact

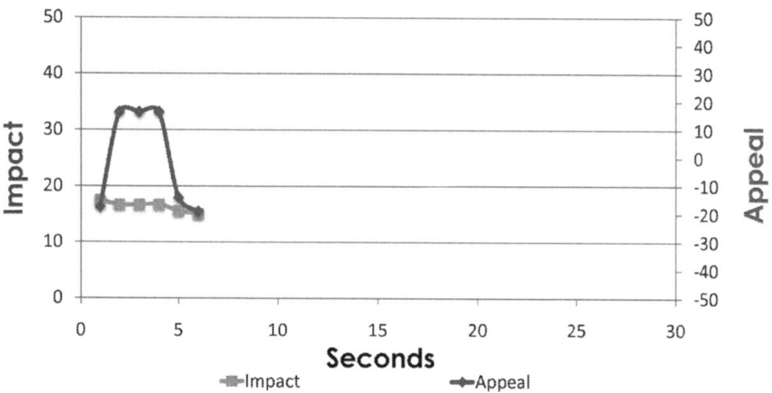

Soft and warm, not bellicose: Edwards connects. But the moment he becomes just another politician with a big, complicated plan, voters tune him out. A commercial that at first draws voters in, soon leaves them cold.

It's hardly as personal and warm as the version of Edwards voters initially experience. Even worse, that version never returns. In place of the kindly Edwards, the version of Edwards that comes back on screen after the Plan is introduced is somebody whose voice rises in anger and whose rhetoric becomes more heated. Consequently, voters have no significant emotional response during the remainder of this spot.

On other occasions, in speeches in particular, Edwards learned to be more intimate. His remarks were peppered with specific stories about people he had met on the campaign trail. But any slight adjustments he made paled in comparison to the wholesale transformation that I saw Clinton accomplish in a speech in Dover, New Hampshire.

There, at a Clinton rally immediately following her misty-eyed talk with female supporters just down the road in Portsmouth, I witnessed a far different Clinton from the one I'd been watching on TV for months. Gone was the smirk. That was the first thing I noticed when Clinton finally took the stage. Yes, the results from Iowa had shattered her confidence. But to imagine ever seeing Clinton without her trademark smirk was just amazing to me, as was the degree to which it remained subdued throughout the rest of the campaign. Even somebody as disciplined as Clinton couldn't, I believe, have simply been able to *will* the smirk off her face so completely. And I say that no matter what amount of body language coaching she might have been receiving.

Next, as Clinton spoke I noticed how much she had slowed her delivery style. Sadness, as in the disappointment of losing in Iowa, will slow you down. But Clinton still seemed feisty enough. So a loss of energy wouldn't fully explain the change.

Instead, I believe that Clinton had come to recognize that speed kills. Talk too fast, and the audience can't grasp what you're saying, let alone absorb it and get emotionally caught up in it. In other words, the joke that has to be explained to you is never as funny as the joke you just get on your own. **To be on-emotion, one needs to allow time for the emotions to be felt and absorbed both by oneself and others**. Otherwise, they won't really register or be conveyed authentically and, therefore, won't have an impact. Perhaps aware of and incorporating that reality, the new Clinton was speaking at only half the rate of her previous policy wonk self.

The crowning touch, though, was that Clinton was now taking questions from the audience. Belatedly perhaps, Clinton had realized that she had put too much distance between herself and her audience of voters. Moreover, she allowed the questions to go on and on, as if to say this is truly a conversation.

In the final analysis, no doubt Clinton's misty-eyed video on YouTube and reports of it in the media made something of a difference. The same is true of working class voters getting under-reported in the sampling polls.[21] But surely so did this new, slower, softer, more open Clinton. That version of the candidate overcame Obama's reported 8% average lead the day before the primary, leading Bob Woodward, on CNN, to call traditional survey methods nothing less than "garbage."[22]

What's the take-away? As Edwards hopefully learned, don't rush and don't shout. Intimacy breeds an emotional connection. Provide both literal close-ups of your face as well as emotional *close-ups* if you want to be on-emotion. It works in Hollywood, and after a century of films they certainly know a thing or two about what it takes to get the audience to care.

DYNAMIC: THE BELLOWING BULL'S DOWNFALL

While relative speed matters in communicating with others, so does variability in a candidate's vocal pitch and volume. In fact, in everything variety enhances the audience's likelihood of response and enjoyment. But let's start with *pitch*, something voice coach Susan Miller analyzed by listening to 12 different candidates.[23] By doing so, Miller discovered that Clinton provided the greatest variability, Paul second most, and Romney the least. In fact, Romney was far enough behind the others that it's fair to say the guy is plagued by being monotone.

Now at first blush, the implication of that finding might not seem like much. But in reality, it's huge and here's why. In emotional terms, being monotone doesn't mean you're steady and consistent. It means you're asleep. It means you're not a part of the universe, where ebb and flow is natural.

Romney's monotone signaled a lack of authenticity and meant he was inevitably off-emotion. That's because **emotions are dynamic, unlike lingering moods. Emotions are little mini-dramas, happening quickly, then gone, as people intuitively grasp that a goal's at stake.** A monotone Romney is really the equivalent of Romney's other most notable delivery mannerism: an endless, high-tide social smile too unreal to believe.

Meanwhile, as to *speed*, Dodd was the fastest by a long shot, with Kucinich a distant second and Paul the slowest. You begin to see why Paul made a great speechmaker during the campaign. Slow enough to let the feelings sink in, Paul also demonstrated variety and kept the audience emotionally awake by emphasizing values and principles.

Now, Miller didn't include *volume* in her vocal analysis of the candidates. But after listening to all the candidates give their stump speeches in person, I would say Dodd takes the booby prize for being consistently the loudest and without much variety. (How can you introduce variety when you're going so fast?) All in all, I soon took to calling the loud and fast Dodd the "Bellowing Bull."

Always angry, Dodd demonstrates a corollary to the principle that to be authentically on-emotion requires ebb and flow. And it's this: **to be constantly on-emotion ends up being the same as being off-emotion**.

In an inverse sort of way, Dodd the Bellowing Bull was like Romney the Monotone. Always loud and angry, Dodd was, I believe from facial coding, genuine enough (certainly far more so than Romney's happy, social smile). Again and again, Dodd expressed his concerns about the erosion of the Constitution and people's civil rights in convincing terms. But neither candidate made voters feel very much in response to them because there wasn't enough variety to spur reciprocal, transitory feelings.

UNDERSTANDABLE: PHONE TAG

Proven again and again in business, good, even great advertising can't necessarily save you. But it sure can help. Clinton was hardly a mediocre candidate. She had knowledge, experience, fortitude and a vast array of contacts. But she did have her limitations. The first of the two Clinton spots I'll discuss next was meant to offset her lack of likeability.

Like the "3 A.M." spot I'll also discuss, "Invisible" owes much of its effectiveness to keeping the concept singularly focused. Showing Clinton able to connect with people was the obvious goal, and it generally worked.

"Invisible" secured more response, more emotional data points than all but two of the other Democratic commercials we tested: a call-for-good-government spot by Obama, and a clean energy spot by Richardson. Even better, however, "Invisible" surpassed both of those in terms of generating higher appeal scores. They came as Clinton appeared on screen with farmers, working mothers, children, and the like.

But there was something about our results that would have disturbed the Clinton camp: it took a long time for viewers to warm up to her. After a first data point, almost 25 seconds elapsed before the next one. By then, Clinton had been seen not just walking with a farmer (a scene that generated her first data point), but also in front of a crowd, with children, a factory worker, a mother. Finally picturing her with a baby to accompany the phrase "affordable childcare" helped her break through again emotionally.

Perhaps even worse, during the last ten seconds of "Invisible"—when Clinton is in the foreground again—the emotional data points disappear. In other words, the results showed that voters weren't emotionally energized by Clinton. On her own they found her less than compelling, suggesting that her emotional connection with the public could be tenuous at best.

In contrast, the "3 A.M." spot came much later in the campaign, airing in March during the crucial Texas primary. By then, Clinton had been through an awful lot. There were all the public doubts about her vote in favor of the Iraq war ("had she been "naïve" to trust Bush?" CNN's Wolf Blitzer asked during one debate). There was also her husband, Bill, repeatedly erupting at Obama. A puffy-eyed, red-faced, finger-wagging ex-president on the loose in South Carolina and elsewhere was a spectacle nobody had expected. Moreover, there was Clinton's assumption that she would put the Democratic nomination on ice on Super Tuesday, only to watch Obama sweep the next 11 contests.

That was already plenty of drama.

But there was still much more to come. There would be Clinton's exposure for reimagining her peaceful landing at a Bosnian airstrip in 1996 as an event complete with sniper fire. The battle for delegates would likewise subject her to ridicule. A George Will column mocked her for trying every mathematical trick in the book to change the inevitable outcome. Maybe she would return us to days of old, he suggested, and count every African-American vote as a 3/5th vote.[24] Unfazed, Clinton traveled to Dade County, Florida, the site of the contested "hanging-chad" ballots in 2000, to dramatize to the party faithful the new political injustice she was suffering from. There she would plead her case that denying her the full slate of Michigan delegates was akin to denying her the kind of basic rights lost in Robert Mugabe's Zimbabwe.[25]

Yes, high drama, all of it.

In the meantime, there was "3 A.M."—a commercial so effective that this spot alone helped Clinton slow, if not quite block, Obama's momentum. Here's the on-emotion anatomy of how and why it works.

Who's Calling, Dear?

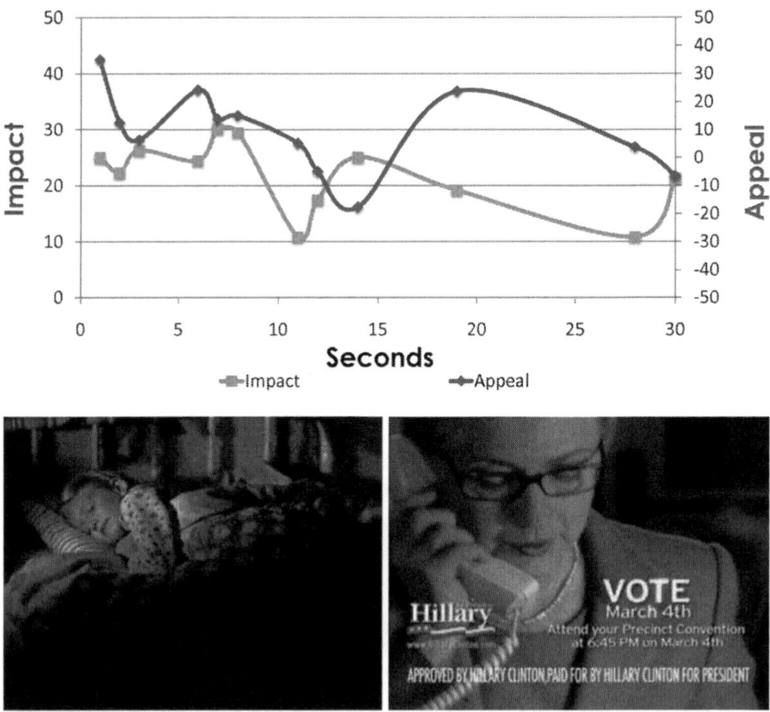

Clinton's "3 A.M." spot was one of only four primary season TV spots that managed to inspire swings in appeal that could, when appropriate, be as captivating as the political equivalent of riding on a rollercoaster. The Biden and Richardson spots weren't able to sustain their momentum. Only McCain's "Issue Alert" was likewise able to use the threat of danger to keep viewers engaged throughout the spot.

For starters, there are two solid high appeal scores, coming both early and late. The early one occurs when viewers see kids safe asleep in bed, with an echo of that scene nearly 20 seconds later. In between, the Clinton team has forcefully delivered its implicit message: Obama can't be trusted with your security. Like McCain's anti-Romney spot, the appeal scores go ever downward—but even more so than in McCain's spot—as a ringing phone and a script that talks about the need for tested, proven leadership gets delivered.

How high are the stakes? So high the appeal score suitably slips to its lowest, most negative point as the script adds that Clinton "knows the military." The inference here is that even more warfare could be part of the country's future, and voters respond with concern.

Clinton herself doesn't make an appearance in "3 A.M." But there is a lookalike, shown on a phone as Clinton's name appears on screen. In addition, Clinton's own very distinct voice comes in at exactly the 28th second when the next to last emotional data point registers—with *positive* appeal. Let's put this accomplishment in context. Consider the fact that of the 29 spots my company tested during the primary season, less than 30% of them spurred an emotional data point during the spot's crucial final five seconds.

In other words, the Clinton spot closed the deal by linking her candidacy with the story line proceeding her voice and name entering the picture. Unlike other spots, here Clinton's candidacy strikes voters as emotionally relevant and appealing.

Furthermore, Clinton's goal of implicitly painting Obama as too unproven a candidate to enter the White House was made and, better yet, made cleanly. Like all great advertising, what "3 A.M." accomplishes is to **enable viewers to put the story together themselves on a more subconscious level**. It enables viewers to close the loop internally, subconsciously, emotionally, with the kind of power that only comes from a compact execution.

In a game of phone tag, Obama was now "it." The onus had been placed on him to assure voters he was up to the job.

VISUALLY-DRIVEN: A SENSE OF PLACE

The first time I heard Obama speak in person, at a labor rally in Cedar Rapids, Iowa in August 2007, I was stunned. I came expecting to hear transcendent prose from Obama, already heralded as a great speaker because of his famous speech at the Democratic National Convention in Boston in 2004. Instead, the man on stage in front of me that evening sounded halting and tired. In a word, his delivery was *flat*—especially compared to the pep shown by Clinton and Edwards.

It worsened. Obama had barely headed into the body of his remarks when a man sitting a dozen or so rows from the stage began heckling him. Suddenly, the man yelled in a voice clearly audible to me a dozen rows away: "You've never worked a day in your life." It was an accusation I would think of again and again in the months ahead as the charge of elitism began to dog Obama's campaign.

In time, Obama's speech-making would become more reliable and I would hear many superb speeches from him. The heckler apparently saw Obama as a greenhorn, privileged slacker. But my sense of Obama would gravitate to something else instead: a sense of Obama as sometimes arrogant, sometimes aloof, but also a figure of potential greatness and already dignified by considerable gravitas.

Some of that gravitas came unwillingly. After all, here you had an African-American leader who frequently invokes the memory of Martin Luther King, Jr. and John and Bobby Kennedy, all of them slain. Moreover, there were concerns for Obama's physical safety, as acknowledged by his wife, Michelle, when she said on *60 Minutes*: "I don't lose sleep over it, because the realities are that . . . [as a black man] Barack can get shot going to the gas station."[26]

Add in Clinton's comment in South Dakota about continuing her efforts because Bobby Kennedy "was assassinated in June in California."[27] Also Huckabee's bad joke at the National Rifle Association convention about how Obama would scramble onto the floor if somebody aimed a gun at him, and what do we have? A certain street credibility accrues to Obama, not only as a black man, but also as a leader prepared to risk his life for higher office.

That alone would be substantial. But there's more. Like other great leaders, Obama understands the value of creating a strong sense of place. Michael Deaver did it for Reagan. I'm talking here about the settings he chooses. Obama traveled to Springfield, Illinois's Old State Capitol house to wrap himself in the tradition of Lincoln when he announced his candidacy. Then when he spoke of racism after the Reverend Wright videos began to light up the internet, Obama chose as his setting a place in Philadelphia across the street from where the Founding Fathers launched "America's improbable experiment in democracy." Then in declaring that the Democratic nomination was his, Obama chose to speak in St. Paul, where he reminded the audience "in just a few short months, the Republican Party will arrive ... with a very different agenda."

The choice of those settings might seem easy and simple, hardly a stroke of genius. And yet consider that "change agent" Clinton launched her campaign from her sofa, sitting in a townhouse inside the Beltway. Or that the same evening Obama was declaring victory in St. Paul, McCain tried to crash his party by giving a speech in a setting that looked like an air force base hangar or worse.

Location matters. Half the brain is devoted to processing visuals. So imagery can certainly influence elections.

How we as voters receive such imagery can vary, of course. Words alone can evoke mental pictures, an ability that during the primary season favored Huckabee over Romney, for instance. Huckabee drew on Biblical stories while Romney was accustomed to relatively abstract, corporate-speak. But the primary medium for imagery remains TV spots, and here the list of which images had the power to stick in the mind during the primary season gets thin.

Among the 29 spots we tested, there are some good, even great spots. Biden's trapped, hole-in-the-ground image comes to mind. For Clinton, there's the young woman beaming in "Invisible" as she takes in the realization that a woman could be president. Richardson's New Mexico comeback spot opens with a scene of him walking fast, a man of action. McCain's anti-Romney spot shows the former Massachusetts governor standing there with what looks like a foolish grin on his face.

Those are images that influence decisions. Then there are all the moments of video that do nothing and aren't memorable. Of the 29 TV spots we tested, nearly a third of them had five or fewer emotional data points.

Finally, there are the unfortunate images that undermine a campaign. Kucinich prancing around to prove that there aren't "any strings" attached to his candidacy comes to mind here. Or Obama filmed talking to a room of supporters in which he swivels his head to make eye contact with people so frequently that he begins to resemble one of those bobble-heads given away at baseball games.

But perhaps the worst example of an off-emotion image comes from a Giuliani TV spot. The spot was generally on-emotion, with negative appeal generated as Giuliani disparaged Clinton and MoveOn.org for criticizing General David Petraeus, the U.S. Iraq commander. Those negative dips in appeal were, as intended, occurring when Clinton was shown on screen. But there was one major exception. That's the dip that occurred in second 17 as Petraeus appears on screen for the second time. What's wrong? Shadowed by a pair of physically larger soldiers, the combat-fatigue wearing, relatively tiny Petraeus brings to mind the infamous image of Michael Dukakis riding atop a tank in 1988.

Why should such a tactical, execution-oriented slip-up like that conclude this section on communications? That's because the poetry—as well as the devil—is always in the details. Showing, instead of telling, works best.

As Obama has figured out, the setting matters. The imagery you evoke matters. **Figure out an arresting visual, and use it to anchor your story, solving the problem visually**. By speaking in Philadelphia adjacent to where the Founding Fathers met, Obama made the Reverend Wright controversy look trivial by comparison to building a society based on the proposition that all of us are created equal. In contrast, the problem with Giuliani's spot attacking Clinton is that in its presentation of Petraeus it visually *creates* a problem for itself.

CONCLUSION

Being on-emotion in communications means two things most of all: protecting and, if possible, enhancing *credibility*, while also reaching out to people in a *compelling* way. Without an offer that's viewed as credible, nothing is possible. Clinton's TV spots, on balance, performed better than Obama's. Likewise, she won pretty much every debate based on rational, talking points. But by re-imagining her Bosnian airfield landing, she verbally undercut much of what her other communications had accomplished and contributed to survey results showing that 60% of Americans consider her "untrustworthy."[28]

Other candidates like Romney and Giuliani likewise had problems with their core brand identity, making communications more problematic. So Romney could spend all the money he wanted on advertising and get, as he did, almost no emotional response that registered as solidly positive in our testing. Meanwhile, because he lacked values-based emotional rapport with the party's base, Giuliani was never on-emotion. Instead, he spent over $3 million in direct mail in New Hampshire and ran almost 3,000 TV spots in Florida to no effect because creating awareness alone isn't remotely related to creating a feeling of loyalty.[29]

Making communications compelling is the other half of the equation. People think in images, not words, and yet most of the 29 spots we tested never really even attempted to leverage that scientific fact. Instead, hamstrung by both budgets and a lack of imagination, most campaigns settled for candidates sitting at desks, standing in front of flags or nondescript backdrops, while talking in abstract *policy-ese*. Well, people love leaders, not bureaucrats.

Part Three:

THE GENERAL ELECTION

5
THE GENERAL ELECTION

Scorecard & Forecast

OVERVIEW

When the primary season was all said and done, what was left? The answer is almost total surprise. In the Republican party, the nomination fight was supposed to drag on, perhaps all the way to the convention. But once the actual voting started, McCain soon became the obvious eventual winner as he benefited most from the collapse of both the Giuliani and Thompson campaigns.

Over on the Democratic side, the pundits and pollsters were no more accurate. Clinton's anticipated coronation became an epic battle with Obama. That Clinton would transform herself from an inside-the-Beltway queen into Norma Rae on steroids was a fallback strategy new to even her own advisors.

In the end, the general election has come down to a contest between two men who, in many ways, couldn't be more different. One is the son of a studious mother whom Obama has described as an Adlai Stevenson-type liberal. Obama would become a good student himself and a teetotaler in contrast with his Kenyan father, who suffered from a drinking problem.[1] The other man is the son and grandson of U.S. Navy admirals, but at Annapolis drew more demerits than praise. To understand McCain a little better, it's worth noting that his mom is the daughter of an Oklahoma oil wildcatter and agreed to get married in a bar in Tijuana, Mexico.[2] Improvisation runs in McCain's veins.

Which man *will* become president? At chapter's end, I'll make a prediction despite the risk of unforeseen variables. But first let's look at which man *should* become president, based on being best able to handle the emotional dynamics of leadership, branding and communications.

THE THREE TOP-TEN LISTS AS SCORE CARDS

Note that the lists are discussed in their rank order of priority. Again, for full descriptions of the items in these lists, see Appendicies A through C.

Emotional Dynamics of Leadership: Top Ten Attributes

Obama wins in four attribute categories, and McCain in three others. But the big question is whether McCain's key advantage—being more trustworthy—is enough to offset Obama's advantage of being more forward-looking. Government bureaucrats and company managers are asked to handle *what is*. From our leaders, however, we expect to learn about *what will be*, suggesting that Obama has the edge here. Note that the attributes to follow are listed in their rank order of priority.

1. **Inspiring**—Advantage: **split**.
   Each candidate can inspire his own partisan audience. Obama does so mostly through eloquent speeches; McCain inspires autobiographically, based on his experiences in Viet Nam. McCain's a genuine hero, an archetypal role whose allure can't be dismissed even in an era as cynical as ours. Each is readily identified with an emotion he owns. For Obama, it's hope. For McCain it's anger feeding into a determination to achieve success (as he defines it).

2. **Trustworthy**—Advantage: McCain.
   Both candidates have adjusted, evolved, or, frankly, *changed* their positions at times. The McCain of 2008 isn't the same as in 2000, and not even necessarily the same as in 2007 as he seeks support from the Republican party's right wing.[3] Meanwhile, Obama has recently run as more of a centralist. So why does this attribute favor McCain? His emotions show more readily (mostly anger). As a result, he seems more immediate, more honest, as if constitutionally unable to suppress his true feelings. In other words, McCain's so *off-emotion* given his inability to suppress his anger that he ends up being *on-emotion* in regard to authenticity.

3. **Forward Looking—**Advantage: **Obama**.
   Obama has shown himself to be more adaptive in general as well as in specifics, such as using the internet. As Obama himself has acknowledged, he self-consciously avoids locking himself in to the status quo or a set way of handling matters. He's committed to avoid repeating what he heard were his father's career failings as an inflexible, opinionated bureaucrat in Kenya.[4]

4. **Confident**—Advantage: **split**.
   Both candidates are confident of their abilities. While McCain is feisty and given to vows like "we will never surrender," Obama was, from an early age, reassured by his mother that he was unique and special. Moreover, Obama was told by his maternal grandfather that confidence is the key "to a man's success,"[5] a lesson Nixon would have endorsed given his sense that American voters like "winners."

5. **Stable—**Advantage: **Obama**.
   McCain's temper is a well known factor, made fun of in political cartoons and noted by most everyone. In contrast, Obama is downright serene, cerebral, and generally not given to strong emotional displays. In motivational terms, security comes first. McCain promises security from *external*, foreign threats. But voters may wonder: what if his lack of stability means that McCain poses an *inside* threat?

6. **Unselfish**—Advantage: **McCain**.
   At a macro level, Obama is more unselfish given his fair-minded desire for America to move beyond partisan wrangling. On a more personal, micro level, however, McCain wins handily because he showed tremendous loyalty by refusing to be released early, ahead of soldiers imprisoned longer by the North Vietnamese. Obama's "You're likeable, enough" comment to Clinton during the New Hampshire debate was decidedly *off-emotion* for him. It also underscored the difficulty he occasionally has being generous. Voters will favor the candidate who seems most willing to look out for them.
7. **Cooperative**—Advantage: **Obama**.
   Obama has been far better at creating a broad, cohesive campaign structure. His primary season advice to staffers was not to get either too up or down regarding the day-to-day twists and turns of a campaign. By contrast, McCain's most naturally a solo artist. Unlike Dwight Eisenhower, McCain runs for the president as a war hero who never really directed others and is most comfortable winging it. Obama versus McCain sets up a classic contrast here, and the chance to learn whether American voters will favor collective effort in a time of struggle or the spirit of individualism that McCain embodies.
8. **Vitality**—Advantage: **split**.
   Obama has youth in his favor but can get tired and peevish. In turn, McCain tires without accepting that he should cut himself some slack. (At the second Republican debate, held at the Ronald Reagan Library, McCain looked like he was propping himself up with his elbows). Still it's hard to count out McCain when it comes to energy level. This is a guy, after all, who got skin cancer as a result of relentlessly campaigning door to door in the mid-day Arizona sun.[6]

9. **Accessible**—Advantage: **McCain**.
McCain is generally more available to the press and is also more spontaneous. Voters can get the sense they're seeing him, warts-and-all. In contrast, Obama is more aloof, distant, and detached, as if this native Hawaiian is truly an island onto himself. In romance and politics alike, we swoon for a person to whom we feel closest.

10. **Positive**—Advantage: **Obama**.
Obama's entire positioning is a matter of hope and optimism. He's gone from success to success. McCain is almost the opposite in outlook. He practically seems to relish being a sour puss, and can be as acerbic as his former U.S. Senate colleague, Bob Dole, another injured war veteran. Just 12 years ago, American voters passed on putting Dole into office, a man temperamentally cut from the same cloth and experience as McCain. Will memories of Dole's losing effort make McCain look equally forlorn?

VICE PRESIDENTIAL OPTIONS: WHO'S NEXT IN LINE?

Intimately related to presidential leadership is deciding on a running mate. In every race, that choice gives voters insight into the leadership style, political calculations and personal values of a nominee. But this time around, the choices are generally agreed to be more crucial than usual. That's because of concerns the vice president might inherit the White House in case Obama was assassinated or McCain was forced out of office due to terminally ill health.

In the admittedly brief profiles to follow, I haven't sought to analyze the policy views or credentials and experience of the various vice presidential options. Instead, my focus is on using facial coding to analyze how each option might emotionally reinforce or balance the nominee's own personality type. One final note: the options selected for study were based on having cross-indexed news stories speculating about who is on Obama's and McCain's short lists.

Republican options include:

Mitt Romney—As the economy falters, this option is probably looking better and better to some of the McCain team, in rational terms. But emotionally this option doesn't work well, as the two men don't like each other. Their faces show it. Allying himself with somebody he dislikes will undercut McCain's brand, which is built on integrity.

Tim Pawlenty—Minnesota's governor has a bit of a temper himself, which is most evident when he tightly presses his lips together in annoyance. Adding a younger, but emotionally similar white male to the ticket doesn't provide much diversity. If he's chosen however, at least McCain and Pawlenty will understand each other well.

Charlie Crist—Florida's governor has eyebrows that lift often as he emphasizes his statements. There's also a fair amount of smiling, which sometimes gets mixed either with contempt or else the corners of the mouth turning down in a frowning, grimace sort of smile. In other words, Crist doesn't merely grin like some clueless, "happy camper." He's smoother than McCain, and would probably make a good emotionally balancing addition to the ticket.

Tom Ridge—This former Pennsylvania governor and former Assistant to the President for Homeland Security is a long-time friend of McCain, but differs from McCain in how he emotes. In Ridge's case, his eyebrows work over-time, lifting for emphasis as he speaks. He also raises his upper lip often in subtle signs of disgust. In short, Ridge gives off the impression of a battle-hardened professional politician who's seen it all and isn't any more likely to indulge in the "warm-and-fuzzy" than McCain is.

Rob Portman—Most recently, Portman was the Director of the Office of Budget and Management for George W. Bush. He's also a former U.S. Congressman from Ohio. In emotional terms, Portman's most common expression is that his lower lip pushes down and out in a sign of bitter disgust. When he smiles, slight anger or contempt often gets shown as well. He would appear more steady and camera-friendly if he didn't blink so much, which can indicate discomfort.

Carly Fiorina—My company was once asked to facially code the former CEO of Hewlett-Packard for an investment firm. What I saw then is essentially what I and voters can see now: Fiorina's eyebrows lower and her mouth tightens in anger. She's no stranger to showing contempt. While she would diversify a McCain ticket by gender, age and experience, she wouldn't add much variety in emotional terms.

Democratic options include:

Hillary Clinton—Whether Obama chooses Clinton remains the big question. Temperamentally, they're never quite on the same page. It's her social smiles versus his true smiles, her anger versus his vexation, her contempt versus his tendency to tilt his head back, as if avoiding the fray she relishes. If Clinton's chosen, it puts the lie to the Obama brand strategy of promising something new and takes his candidacy decidedly *off-emotion*. Perhaps political expediency will overrule that concern.

Tim Kaine– The Virginia governor is a friend of Obama's and the son of a former U.S. Senator notable for his support of civil rights. From the little I've seen of Kaine, what strikes me is that he smiles fairly often but they are tighter smiles than Obama's more expansive true smiles. Equally common is for Kaine to lift his chin so that his mouth forms an upside-down smile, signaling feelings like anger, disgust and sadness. Kaine is in short a mixture of happiness and resolve, temperamentally not so far from Obama's own nature.

Wesley Clark—I facially coded Clark on stage and in the debates for the 2004 race. The guy I saw didn't take to politics readily. His smiles were weak, and fear and surprise reactions occasionally took over his face. For a retired U.S. Army general and former Rhodes Scholar, he seems remarkably unsure of himself and unlikely to put voters at ease, much less inspire confidence.

Claire McCaskill—A U.S. Senator from Missouri, she is in emotional terms a perfect compliment to Obama. She would reinforce his strengths and offset his weaknesses. McCaskill has a great true smile, and is at ease with herself. Her candor is refreshing and not biting. When she's against something, her upper lip may rise in a sign of disgust, but not without a mitigating smile. In summary, she's warm and shows no signs of being aloof.

Evan Bayh—This U.S. Senator from Indiana doesn't emote very much, and when he does it's mostly to show the slightest of smiles, a nod, or a little tightening of the lips. He's a smooth talker, but not exciting to watch. For the white male voter, his presence on the ticket might be reassuring. However, adding Bayh to the ticket represents an off-emotion choice because he's not very emotional.

Janet Napolitano—The current governor of Arizona is neither emotionally flat nor warm. Traces of annoyance are probably her most common expression. Her eyebrows will knit together, and her mouth sets tight. Brief smiles and hints of disgust and sadness round out the picture. Napolitano creates the impression of a politician who's warm enough to be a suitable on-emotion choice for Obama, while helping to inoculate him against charges of being a "softie" without enough substance.

Emotional Dynamics of Branding: Top Ten Objectives

Obama has been far more effective than McCain has in building a brand for himself. So it's no surprise that Obama is favored in four categories and McCain in only one. However, the other five evenly split categories include four of the top five brand objectives—all except for the aspirational objective, which tilts to Obama's advantage. Let's assume the election functions as a referendum on Obama: who *is* he? Then the Senator from Illinois will want to solidify and protect his brand image to leverage this advantage.

1. **Faithful**—Advantage: **split**.
   Both candidates have sought to make honesty a hallmark of their respective campaigns. In McCain's case, ever since his association with the Keating Five scandal, he's seemed intent on trying to bolster his reputation for integrity. In Obama's case, his campaign slogan indicates the premium he places on being perceived as authentic and believable. Overall, the candidates are equally on-emotion regarding the public's desire for a president they can trust. They both know that without integrity, their personal brands won't have staying power now, or in the White House.
2. **Reflective**—Advantage: **split**.
   On a thematic level, both candidates equally emphasize values that matter to their party and its supporters. In McCain's case, those beliefs include: honor, integrity, and service. In Obama's case, the focus shifts to tolerance, fairness, and progress. Given that those values also reflect the values each candidate was raised with, they can speak to them with conviction, depriving either one of an advantage here.
3. **Aspirational**—Advantage: **Obama**.
   McCain is by his nature an individualist and, on the campaign trail, better suited to being a counterpuncher than a candidate who speaks in visionary terms. By contrast, as a former community organizer in Chicago's struggling south side, where the country's biggest group of African-Americans reside, Obama has long been accustomed to bolstering people's self-identities.

Affirming what America *could* become is at the very core of what motivates Obama to run for president.

4. **Promising—**Advantage: **split.**
The role of myth in McCain's brand centers on his personal story of courage and heroism as a prisoner in North Vietnam. The implication is that the strength he showed then will now be used on the country's behalf. That leading by individual example model suits McCain's save-yourself philosophy. In contrast, Obama counters with an equally strong myth: a vision of America as a place where a group of people are still striving to form a more perfect union. Heavily influenced by Lincoln, Obama and his dream of communal uplift also bears a similarity to Reagan's talk of America as a "shining city on a hill" example for the world at large.

5. **Exclusive—**Advantage: **split.**
This objective is again equally realized because both candidates strive to make their potential supporters feel like they belong to an inner circle of noble, true believers. For McCain, drawing an "us" versus "them" distinction is easy and natural for a man who routinely disparages others. Obama's instincts are quite different. While McCain has a history of mixing it up, Obama typically avoids conflict. He speaks out against polarization and favors a post-partisan America. Obama calls on his supporters to dare to hope, and in doing so implicitly suggests that McCain's gritty realism is both self-limiting and self-defeating.

6. **Gender-Sensitive** Advantage: **Obama.**
McCain's a man's man and the campaign trail events that I've witnessed have felt like old-time VFW gatherings. The gender gap that's meant male voters favor the GOP while female voters favor the Democrats is likely to be in full force again this year. Of the two candidates, Obama can relate to men, in part, through his enjoyment of sports. (For instance, ESPN's *Sports Center* is his favorite show.)[7] Unlike McCain, however, Obama also exhibits the more traditionally feminine trait of being conciliatory. That makes Obama uniquely able to reinforce his post-partisan theme by also bridging male/female differences.

7. **Adaptive—**Advantage: **Obama**.
   The McCain brand relies on the candidate's ability to exude steadfastness, even at the risk of appearing rigid. The Obama brand maintains its underlying principles, too, but is otherwise very adaptive, from using the internet well to reflecting the country's changing demographics.

8. **Narrative—**Advantage: **split**.
   Both candidates have published memoirs to establish their life stories in the hearts and minds of voters. Each narrative enjoys its own advantages. McCain's story is more immediate, with greater intensity of detail. Obama's story is more unusual, even exotic, and well told as part of an intellectual journey to understand one's self-identity. It's up to voters now to decide if Obama's story feels too foreign to them to relate to, versus McCain's more old- fashioned story of individual valor and patriotism.

9. **Personable—**Advantage: **McCain**.
   Obama can appear rather aloof, even imperious at times, such as when he tilts his head back and, in effect, looks "down his nose" at others. He can be opaque also, and relishes his privacy. On a media tour of Africa in 2006, for instance, Obama grew tired of his press entourage and wondered aloud where his media advisor was to help him out, saying: "Where is the animal trainer? Where is the whip and chair?"[8] Whereas Obama can become peevish, McCain gets indignant. When he's mad, he's far from charming. But McCain enjoys a slight advantage here because his maverick label gives him a more identifiable and, therefore, more readily grasped personality than Obama, whose projected dreams inspire more emotion than he might personally.

10. **Imagistic—**Advantage: **Obama**.
    Obama has seeded his brand story with allusions to Martin Luther King, Jr., the Kennedys, Lincoln, Gandhi and other great leaders. McCain alludes to Reagan and, on rare occasions, Teddy Roosevelt. Otherwise, he hasn't drawn on many cultural icons, and depends on military symbolism to carry the day.

BRANDED CANDIDATES: WHAT COMES TO MIND?

Smart branding guides which associations get activated in voters' minds regarding a given candidate, and how voters *feel* about those associations. Are the links being made helpful, hurtful or neutral? Do they increase the odds that voters will be able to relate to and endorse a given candidate? Every voter will be different, of course. So no conclusive judgments can be made regarding the brand equity each candidate enjoys.

Nevertheless, what follows is an attempt to capture—and illustrate—some of the associations that might most readily come to mind regarding McCain and Obama. The judgment of whether each association is positive or not is based on how likely it is to be on- or off-emotion given how the candidate has branded himself.

McCain Associations

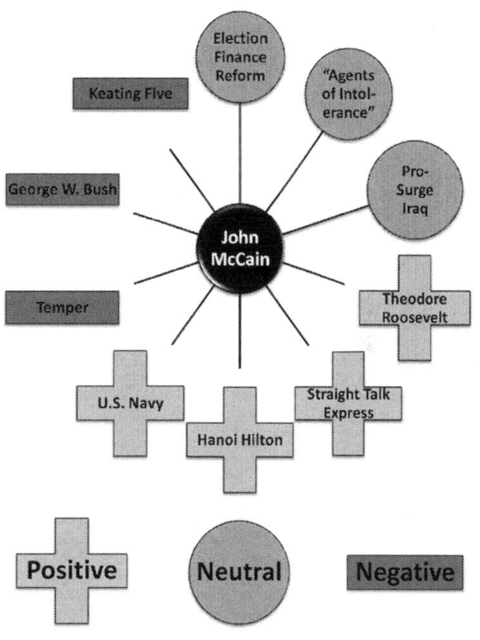

McCain's positives include his Straight Talk Express bus from the 2000 campaign and admiration of the former president Theodore Roosevelt, both of which reinforce his maverick image. His ties to the Keating Five Scandal is exactly contrary, a sign of compliance, of going along with "the system." As a result of that scandal, McCain has identified himself with a need for campaign finance reform (even at the risk of angering many Republicans, who perceive the status quo as an advantage for them due to generally better fundraising abilities).

The other two ambivalent associations regard McCain's famous outburst against the fundamentalists Jerry Falwell and Pat Robertson during the 2000 race as well as his advocacy of a surge of troops in Iraq. Those two associations are neutral, depending on a voter's perspective. In the first case, the association is most likely neutral because McCain has not managed to convince the right wing he's "one of them." Nor has he preserved his independent identity now that he's spoken at Falwell's Liberty University. Regarding Iraq, McCain may be right about the merits of the surge itself. But the general public also associates him with endorsing a war it is now generally against.

Obama Associations

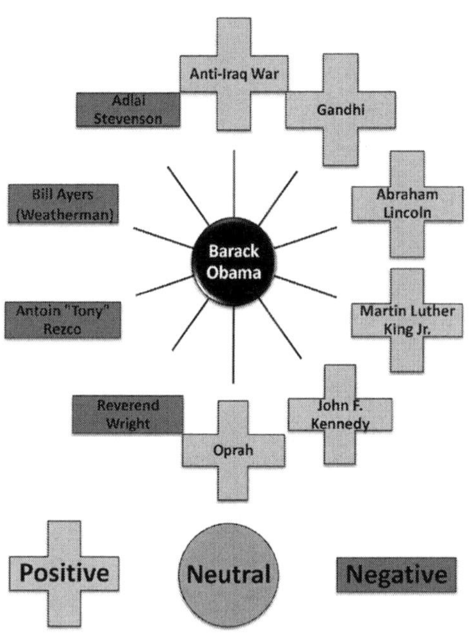

The two Illinois politicians on this brand map illustrate the yin and yang of Obama's branded universe. He could prove to be another Lincoln or else Adlai Stevenson, the classic egghead, who on being told by an adoring fan, "Every intelligent American is voting for you," replied: "Yes, ma'am. But I need a majority." Still being defined in the public's mind, Obama wants voters to see him in the tradition of exalted leaders as well as figures they're comfortable with, like Oprah. The risk is, of course, that he could be pegged by his association with outside-the-mainstream activists like Ayers and Wright, or a corrupt financier like Rezco.

Emotional Dynamics of Communications: Top Ten Goals

Here, McCain has the advantage in five of the categories versus two for Obama. The other three are equally split. Why is that? In essence, the explanation is that McCain's personal story of patriotic heroism in Vietnam is more immediate, more compact and obvious as well as compelling. He's also a natural counter-puncher, ready to go negative like he did in his effective "Issue Alert" commercial attacking Romney on the eve of the New Hampshire primary.

In contrast, none of the TV spots by Obama that my company had previously tested were able to produce a dynamic flow in voters' responses to them. Viewers emotionally abandoned any spot they may have found too wordy and complex. As you'll soon see, however, the latest Obama campaign ad that we tested appears to have reversed that trend.

1. **Hopeful**—Advantage: **Obama**.
   Thanks to his younger, fresher look and uplifting message, Obama is, by a large margin, more on-emotion when it comes to his signature theme of inspiring hope. For McCain, his only real recourse in this case is to run advertising that attempts to puncture Obama's hopefulness without coming across as too negative. McCain's message is that he will make Americans safer, thus selling them on a promise of certainty instead of possibilities for a rosier future.
2. **Relevant**—Advantage: **McCain**.
   McCain best addresses the oldest and strongest of the four core motivations for people:[9] the need to *defend* yourself. His anger is very on-emotion when it comes to striking back against an enemy. Of the other three motivations—acquire, bond, and learn—Obama is stronger in the latter two. But so basic and essential is the defend motivation that it defeats the edge Obama has regarding people's innate desire to draw close to people as well as fulfill their curiosity.
3. **Visually-Driven**—Advantage: **Obama**.
   McCain's TV spots have been as good as or better than Obama's when it comes to using imagery to support his cause. Given the

latest, much improved Obama TV spot, however, it's fair to say the two candidates are equal in advertising terms. But Obama's speechmaking skills enable him to paint more descriptive word-pictures, giving him the overall edge.

4. **Believable**—Advantage: **split**.
   The two candidates seek to make their on-air and stump-speech promises plausible based on overcoming opposing difficulties. In Obama's case, he's sometimes criticized as being light and airy with an offer—hope—that is so vague it creates both the benefit and disadvantage of allowing everyone to project into it what they want. So Obama's communications challenge is to prove he's grounded in pragmatic reality without going off-emotion. In contrast, when McCain warns about foreign threats to America's security, he appears dark and heavy. His challenge is to demonstrate enough lightheartedness that he doesn't scare people about what he might do in the name of defending them. In other words, being too on-emotion (with anger) threatens to make McCain off-emotion as a safe bet to be our president.

5. **Values-Driven**—Advantage: **McCain**.
   His true-blue American story is more concrete than the new, hazier introduction that Obama has been able to write so far. For Obama, the real story will only begin if he wins. At present, Obama still isn't familiar enough to have linked his candidacy to values voters have enshrined in their hearts. Moreover, his vulnerability to charges of elitism threatens to disconnect him from the kind of small-town, rural voters he disparaged in San Francisco.

6. **Understandable**—Advantage: **split**.
   In his soaring speeches, Obama is careful to project a great, overarching purpose to his candidacy: uniting Americans and making progress. In contrast, McCain has a steady stance—that of the reformer. This goal is equally realized because Obama is eloquent but not a very good sound-bite politician, whereas McCain is sincere but handicapped by not being very eloquent, period.

7. **Personalized**–Advantage: **McCain**.
   McCain has got a tangible, pungent personality. You may not like him, but you know who he is. On the other hand, the cerebral Obama is harder to get a grasp of. That's true even though his advertising is working hard and fast to fill in the biographical details. A heartfelt testimonial or other form of tribute to a specific instance of Obama's values in action might help close this gap.
8. **Memorable**—Advantage: **McCain**.
   While Obama will surely have the more lively, creative videos on the internet, McCain is certainly more willing to throw punches that might land hard as the general election approaches. Already, McCain is prepared to challenge Obama's patriotism by questioning his judgment regarding the surge in Iraq. Now, if McCain's comments to the press and negative advertising are deemed to have gone too far, yes, that will hurt him. But when the opposition candidate is as open to being defined as Obama is still, McCain's team has the opportunity it needs.
9. **Dynamic**—Advantage: **split**.
   Given his optimistic nature, Obama will have better luck ending on a high, positive note in his communications. His challenge is not to clutter his message and, therefore, block its flow. McCain's team can offset the energy and positive spirit of the Obama camp with three advantages of its own. The first is a candidate with a compact, compelling personal story. The other two advantages are McCain's well-defined personality, and a willingness to be confrontational, which can give his advertising greater edgy direction and purpose.
10. **Reassuring**—Advantage: **McCain**.
    His military service and longer record of public service, overall, grant McCain more opportunity to assure people that things will be okay under his command. In many ways, the general election is a referendum on whether people can get comfortable enough with Obama to make a leap of faith.

LATEST ADVERTISING: HEAD-TO-HEAD BIOGRAPHIES

As the general election heats up, I wanted to get one last read on how voters are now feeling about the candidates. So my company tested two additional TV spots, focusing not on issues in the headlines but, rather, advertising that seeks to define the candidates in voters' hearts and minds. One autobiographical spot per candidate was chosen, pitting Obama's "Dignity" spot against McCain's "American Reformer."

Voter Response to Obama's "Dignity"

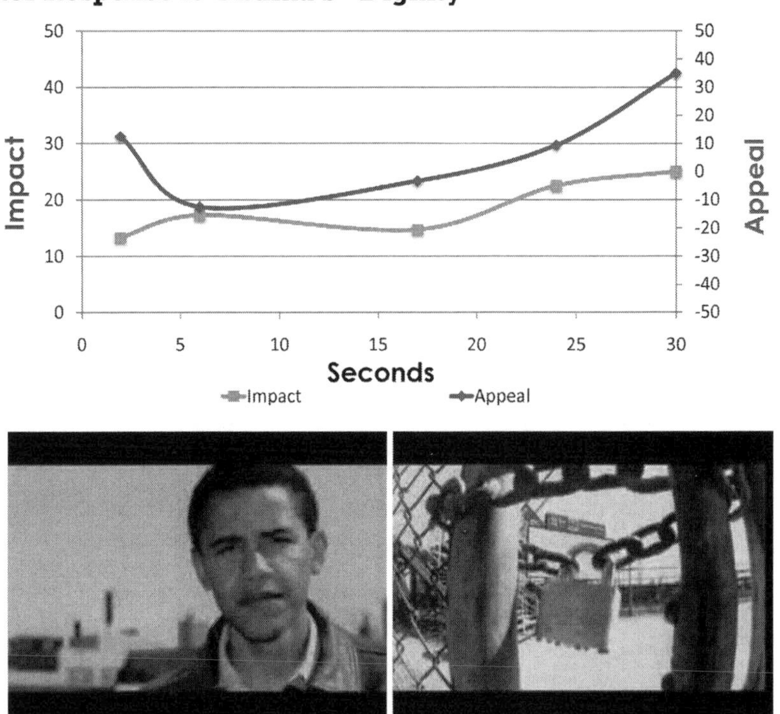

As a result, we found that Obama's "Dignity" engages voters most often at five points during its run, most often with an effective verb choice triggering an emotional response. The first and last points—the ones with the highest appeal score—are when the candidate is on screen. That serves as a strong indication that Obama's personal brand equity is high. The first comes when a photograph of a younger Obama is shown, accompanied by the words "*worked* his way through law school." The last image is of him playfully hugging one older kitchen aide among a crew of female workers.

In between, the points of engagement come in relation to these lines: "helped *lift* neighborhoods," "*passed* tax cuts for workers," wants to "*reward* those companies that create jobs in America." While the commercial doesn't spur a flood of response—and is lacking in impact—it succeeds in securing a steady string of mostly positive reactions. Best of all as far as Obama supporters are concerned, this spot ends on an emotional high note, signaling Obama's likeability.

Voter Response to McCain's "American Reformer"

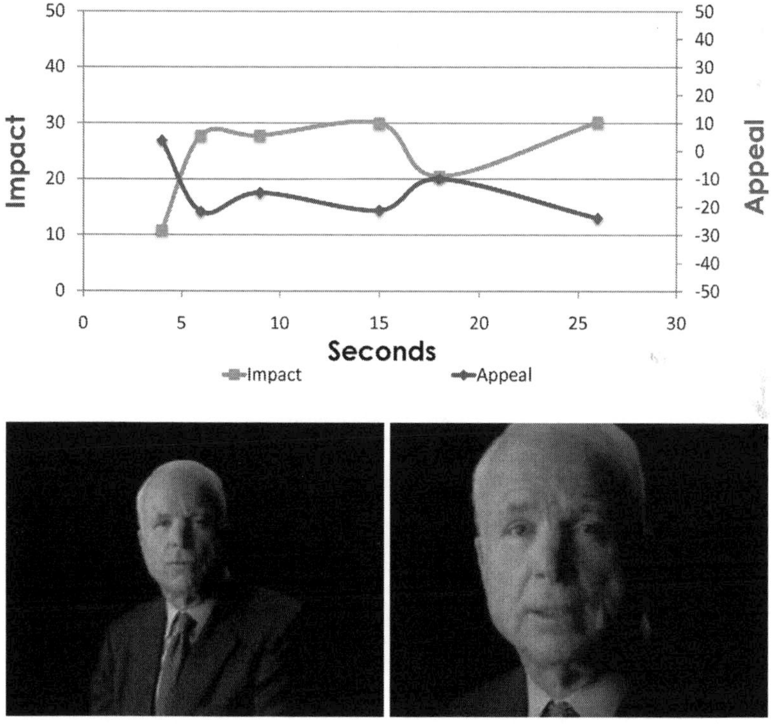

With "American Reformer," the McCain campaign has decided to leverage, rather than hide from, the candidate's reputation for anger. The commercial reprises a standard stump speech segment in which McCain gives reasons why his anger benefits America. In this 30-second version of that segment, McCain inspires an emotional response from voters regarding three ways he's angered people.

Seconds 4 & 6: upset *corporate lobbyists* when he *passed* campaign finance reform

Second 9: made the *Pentagon angry* (by opposing Rumsfeld's plans in Iraq)

Seconds 15 & 18: angered the *big spenders in Congress* . . . by calling for *ethics reform*.

Worrisome for McCain, however, has to be how the voters we tested responded to these three specific issues. Except for when McCain begins by citing his opposition to lobbyists and special interests, every appeal score is low—indicating that the position he's taken isn't inspiring happiness in voters.

Moreover, when McCain says at second 26, "*I love her* [America] enough to make some people angry," the appeal score ties for its lowest point in the test. Oddly enough, that affirmative comment produces a negative emotional response—the inverse of how Obama is received by voters at the end of the "Dignity" spot. Could it be that voters are rejecting McCain personally? Or perhaps they don't like the solutions he's championing in this spot? Or they don't believe that anger is prudent? Those are questions only additional in-depth interviews with voters and the general election tally can answer with more certainty.

What's clear for now, from comparing the results for these two spots, is that Obama is achieving uplift; McCain is not. The confrontational approach showcased in McCain's spot is more impactful but is never emotionally uplifting.

EMOTIONAL FACTORS DRIVING THE ELECTION

Given what brain science has revealed about how people *really* make decisions in life, my predictions about how each candidate could win doesn't revolve around the issues. The Iraq war, the economy, health care, immigration and other vital issues have their place, and at times get referenced here. But that's true only to the extent that those issues, as framed by a candidate, will generate a strong and resounding emotional response in voters. Factors that speak to the heart—like the candidate's vitality, strength and warmth and, yes, skin color and values—can weigh just as heavily. (Since only traditional polling data exists to help discuss many of the following reasons, I cite them here despite concerns about their accuracy.)

Top 10 Reasons Why Obama Wins

10. **Height**—Obama is taller than McCain by seven or eight inches, and in the 20th and 21st centuries the taller candidate has won 70% of the time. Moreover, if elected McCain would be the shortest president in 120 years.[10] Nor is it just in politics that leaders are often tall. Less than 15% of American men are six feet or taller. But in Fortune 500 companies, 58% of all male CEOs are six feet tall or taller.[11] What's the explanation for a trend without any rational defense? The answer could be subconscious and ancient. Perhaps greater height projects dominance, thus reassurance—based on an ancestral advantage for taller hunters able to see across the horizon a little better.

9. **Vitality**—McCain runs the risk of running himself ragged. Confronted by Obama's vast fundraising advantage, McCain is now likely to be forced to compete in all 50 states. Already, I've noticed in some campaign plane video footage a slight tremor in McCain's hands. If McCain ends up looking his age, or worse, that will frighten Americans, who favor youth and who also know the presidency is a physically-demanding job. Obama's boyish freshness gives him a near-term boost, too, because running for the White House is such a grueling process.

8. **Faith**—Here, Obama has two advantages. The first is of his own making. He speaks more comfortably and often about his religious faith than Kerry or Al Gore did. Even more of an advantage, however, is that McCain has turned religion into a neutral factor this time out by not being comfortable or compelling in discussing it. Asked about his religious faith on the campaign trail, McCain will often, for example, tell a story about being treated generously by a North Vietnamese guard one Christmas Day.[12] But it's a stock answer, and he doesn't elaborate. In other words, he might not have anything else to say because religion doesn't appear to play a major role in his life. In past presidential elections, introducing religion into the race has helped the Republicans enjoy more support among church-go'ers. Keeping religion on the sidelines this time around favors Obama.

7. **Urgency**—Republican fundamentalists have typically provided many of that party's campaign volunteers, the ground troops who on Election Day make the last phone calls and drive people to the polls. They have done so out of a genuine sense of urgency about the country's moral direction. This time out, however, young people and the black churches will step up—to the Democrats' advantage. Almost 60% of voters under 30 years of age identify more strongly with Democrats than Republicans, a doubling of the party's advantage among the young since 2004.[13] Simultaneously, other survey data indicates that 89% of African-Americans are highly likely to vote for Obama, with only 3% favoring McCain.[14] Contrast those findings with disarray and disillusionment among Republicans. The net outcome is that the Democrats no longer need to rely on an ever-decreasing number of union members to get out the vote. This time, the party's grass roots efforts will be motivated not by labor, but instead by a labor of love.

6. **Gender**—if the friction with the Clintons continues to heal and Democratic women reconcile themselves to Obama's candidacy, the gender gap may grow even wider. In the last two elections, men voted Republican by better than a 10% margin, while in

2000, but not 2004, women voted Democratic by equal margins. This time Obama looks to be ahead not only with women (by 9%) but also with men (by 4%).[15] McCain's sensibility—a man's man—may play well with some female voters, but it's also likely not to fit the perspective of many career women and soccer moms alike.

5. **War-Weariness**—at present, the U.S. troop surge in Iraq appears to be working. But Afghanistan is heating up with increased levels of violence. To the extent that those two conflicts drag on, or worsen, voters' war fatigue with obscure foreign conflicts favors Obama. At present, only 36% of Americans believe we did the right thing in taking military action against Iraq (while 59% say we should have stayed out).[16] A sense of hopelessness and disillusionment about the reasons for being in Iraq can only help Obama.

4. **Indifference**—McCain is having a hard time rallying the base of Republican voters. At present, only 14% of McCain supporters back him strongly, versus 28% for Obama.[17] Like George Bush, Sr., McCain has a hard time with the "vision thing." His failure to establish a large, overarching reason for his campaign is the strategic equivalent to struggles to make his campaign operations gain cohesion. A second way in which indifference might kill McCain's candidacy is that Hispanic leaders, previously somewhat sympathetic, haven't been quick to forgive him for changing his position by agreeing with his fellow Republicans that border security should take precedence over reforming the country's immigration policies. (The latest poll has Obama leading among Hispanics by 21%.)[18] As a result, that issue alone may cost McCain states like New Mexico and Colorado that already hang in the balance.

3. **Bush**—Everywhere he goes Obama wisely talks of McCain's candidacy as if it would be the equivalent of granting George W. Bush a third term. Given Bush's low approval rating, approximately 30%,[19] that intra-party association puts a millstone around McCain's neck. Obama is safe here because he's so clearly

not cut from the Bush leadership mode, whereas McCain could be seen as sharing Bush's Wild West, cowboy swagger. No one who feels betrayed by Bush's performance in office can readily vote for McCain.

2. **Optimism**—Obama is by far the more optimistic candidate, and when it's all said and done Americans go with hope. Nixon's victory in 1968 is the one big recent exception. But given the events of that year (the Tet Offensive in Viet Nam, assassinations, race riots, etc.), a person who was hopeful that year could easily be accused of being crazy. Remember that Hubert Humphrey was often called the "Happy Warrior." But in seeking to replace LBJ in 1968, he still had to live down his comment from the year before that "Viet Nam is our greatest adventure and what a wonderful adventure it is."

1. **Stoicism**—The country's current economic difficulties greatly worsen McCain's chances of getting elected. Moreover, McCain doesn't have any real experience or knowledge about the economy. Obama doesn't, either. But in McCain's case, his natural, suck-it-up stoicism means he could be seen as insufficiently sensitive to the plight of the economically vulnerable. McCain was quick to distance himself from the comments of his friend and off-and-on-again campaign advisor, former U.S. senator Phil Gramm, who said the country is merely in a "mental recession."[20] Gramm's cavalier attitude is at odds with an AP-Ipsos poll from late June, which finds that eight of ten Americans believe the country is moving in the wrong direction.[21] By association, McCain is at risk of appearing as if he'd rather protect Americans from foreign fighters than from financial pressures that become a matter of protecting home and family.

Top 10 Reasons Why McCain Wins

10. **Capitalism**—Obama has spoken in the past about being essentially repulsed by the "coldness of capitalism."[22] So he has two vulnerabilities here. The first is if he advocates economic policies during the campaign that strike people as naïve, based on a gaffe. The second, lesser risk is that Obama indicates an outside-the-mainstream rejection of capitalism, in favor of Socialist-type solutions, thereby looking more left-wing than may be electable.

9. **Underdog**—Americans generally like to root for the scrappy underdog and at this point the national poll numbers show McCain behind. Aboard his campaign plane, talking with reporters, McCain is often able to use his close-quarters communications skills to good effect. (A notable recent exception would be McCain being asked why healthcare policies often cover erectile dysfunction drugs like Viagra, but not birth control. McCain hemmed and hawed for nearly eight second—even once covering his mouth with his hand, as if to hide—before giving a weak answer.) In general, humor, candor, and accessibility are all qualities that McCain can use to paint himself in a better light than Obama.

8. **Bargainer**—Much of the informal African-American leadership (from Jesse Jackson or Al Sharpton, for example) tends to be more confrontational in approach to white/black relations. (Recently, Obama was criticized by Jackson for "talking down to black people.")[23] Obama isn't a challenger; he's a bargainer, seeking reconciliation. But if new tensions with Reverend Wright were to erupt, provoking resentment and suspicion—a sense that Obama's an appeasing Uncle Tom—then any disconnect between Obama and the black community could lower his support and undercut the huge advantage he expects to enjoy with a key constituency.

7. **Generic**—As the current frontrunner, Obama runs the risk of playing it safe by trying to run out the clock. If he goes too

generic and attempts to be all things to all people by compromising his positions, then he could come across as merely an opportunist. With any candidate that would be a problem. But going generic would be especially bad for Obama because his candidacy is based on being accepted on faith, rather than having a long, proven track record.

6. **Iran**—Now we're into an "if" scenario. There are other global hot spots that could flare up before Election Day and put McCain's foreign policy credentials in the spotlight. North Korea comes to mind. But something involving Iran threatening Israel or Iraq is probably most troubling, and also most likely to make McCain look like the man to affirm the country's status and world image.

5. **Attacked**—Here's another "if" scenario. Should another 9/11-type domestic attack happen, this factor would go from a fourth-ranked factor to most likely the number one reason why McCain would capture the White House. Indeed, a top adviser to McCain, Charlie Black, was quoted in *Fortune* saying that such an attack "certainly would be a big advantage"[24] for McCain. A much more minor version of 9/11, such as infiltrators captured, for instance, might still be enough to put McCain over the top.

4. **Fluff**—According to Gallup polling, among the 39% of Americans who least want Obama to win the White House, nearly 4 in 10 of those people cite Obama's lack of experience.[25] Some people refer to it the "fluff" factor. Other people call it the Commander-in-Chief hurdle. Either way, this factor is the one Clinton highlighted by running her "3 A.M." commercial, asking Americans who they want to have answer the call in case of a crisis.

3. **Patriotism**—Testimony from McCain's co-prisoners in North Vietnam could result in riveting film footage and help sway the undecided. Ever since his remarks at the fundraiser in San Francisco, Obama has been at higher risk of looking like he doesn't affirm the country's heartland. Glitches like that only reinforce inaccurate rumors, such as allegations that he refuses

to say the Pledge of Allegiance. Obama's reserved nature could make it hard for him to affirm adequately his patriotism if challenged by McCain or his supporters.

2. **Aloofness**—By most estimates, Obama needs to win 45% of the white, high-school educated voter segment, and may simply not be able to do so because those voters don't identity with him and begrudge his "elitism." Polls show that 58% of Americans say McCain shares their values, versus 47% for Obama.[26] Because values are emotionally based—as is loyalty—those results are good news for McCain. Furthermore, Obama isn't a candidate who's very good at being a regular guy. So people may not relate to him and accept him as their president. Unless he can overcome the aloof superiority his body language increasingly conveys, Obama could be in trouble. His anthropologist mother might not have done him any favors should he have inherited and exhibit a tendancy to view other people with clinical detachment.

1. **Racism**—This problem is at once the most emotional, most obvious, and least honestly-disclosed reason why Obama may not make it to the White House. An exit poll during the Pennsylvania primary indicated that 18% of Democrats said race matters and that only 63% of them would support Obama in the general election.[27] And that's just among the Democrats. Other analysis has revealed that Obama does best in states with less than 5% or more than 30% of the populace being African-Americans.[28,29] When the percentage falls in between 5-30%, those states are too polarized, yet lacking enough black votes to help him win there. The latest polling numbers available from a *New York Times* and CBS News telephone poll indicate some troubling numbers for Obama. First, 24% of whites say the country isn't ready to elect a black president. Second, 31% of whites have a favorable view of Obama (4% less than McCain.)[30] The big difference is that 9% more whites have an unfavorable view of Obama than they do of McCain. So it may be hard for Obama to make headway among the country's largest segment of voters.

WHERE IS AMERICA HEADED THIS ELECTION DAY?

As you can see from these respective top-ten lists for why each candidate will win the White House, McCain faces longer odds. His list is perhaps more like eight reasons and two prayers. Those two prayers refer, of course, to the two what-if scenarios cited, whereby a foreign or domestic crisis with national security implications will cause voters to flee to the perceived safety of McCain's military experience.

If either candidate wins handily, Obama would seem most likely to be that candidate if no crisis erupts. In general, however, Obama looks at present to be poised for a narrow but historic victory over a rival still capable of deflating him. And that very scenario could definitely happen because McCain's flat, caustic style is the perfect foil to Obama's loftier, gauzy style.

Obama's whirlwind eight-country trip abroad, just completed, serves as an example of how McCain could strike back. "With all the breathless coverage from abroad, and with Senator Obama now addressing his speeches to 'the people of the world,' I'm starting to feel a little left out," McCain retorted the other day. "Maybe you are, too." That kind of counter-punching suits McCain well—so long as he doesn't come across as merely sour.

Between now and Election Day, new developments and surprises will emerge of course. The likelihood that Obama will face racially-charged advertising, not unlike the Swift Boat ads used against Kerry in 2004, is fairly high. The impact of such a onslaught is yet to be seen. Likewise, any number of damaging, even fatal, problems could befall the Republicans, ranging from some blunder by President Bush, to a public temper tantrum or health issue plaguing McCain.

No matter what happens, however, this has already been a fascinating election cycle given all the emotional dynamics at play. In 2004, President Bush ran a negative campaign—as if he was actually the challenger, not the incumbent. He played on people's fears of another 9/11 and also whatever resentments he could stoke using social issues like gay marriage. In 2008, Giuliani tried for a reprise of 2004 by playing the fear card. But his fellow Republicans proved indifferent to him, giving the nod to the most visibly and consistently angry man among all the angry men running this year: McCain.

The Republicans actually had more emotionally moderate, upbeat candidates to choose from. Think of Romney, Huckabee and Thompson. In contrast, the Democrats could count only Obama and, at times, Clinton in that category. But in their final choice of a nominee, the Republicans have gone emotionally heavy (dark and somber), the Democrats the opposite.

A desire for authenticity is what unites the two remaining candidates. Obama dislikes phony routines, and prefers to write his own speeches. Indeed, he is by all accounts not nearly as good at delivering those written by other people. In turn, McCain can barely handle a teleprompter at all and prefers to give off-the-cuff remarks in town-hall type forums where he can improvise and be himself. As longtime McCain aide, Mark Salter, has observed regarding McCain: "Feeling fraudulent is very debilitating to him." The issue of whether McCain being himself is enough to propel him to an upset victory remains one big general election question. Whether Americans get sufficiently comfortable with Obama is another.

In 2004, Kerry seemed immune—too "in his own head"—to grasp the crucial role emotions play in deciding the presidency. Defeat followed, despite an unpopular war and a weak economy.

Whether by instinct or by analyzing the political landscape, Obama has from the very start of his campaign approached matters quite differently. *The Audacity of Hope* forcast the emotional basis of his campaign. In contrast, McCain's willingness to acknowledge his anger in his new TV spot highlights the emotion with which he's most identified.

Surely, the country's Election Day verdict will hinge on many factors. But in emotional terms, the choices poised by Obama and McCain are clear. Americans will be casting ballots this November to resolve whether at this moment in the country's history, hopes and dreams or indignation and resolve feel more on-emotion to them.

APPENDICIES

APPENDIX A:

Top Ten Leadership Attributes

1. **Inspiring**—great leaders excite and motivate us by showing the courage to pursue excellence.
2. **Trustworthy**—being honest and straightforward enables connection because we only like and respect those in whom we can put our faith.
3. **Forward Looking**—emotionally open, value vision; forward-looking leaders are imaginative, intelligent, and independent, and exhibit the only cognitive skill found predictive of success: the ability to sift through the big picture for patterns
4. **Confident**—followers seek reassurance of success; they want to feel safe; in desiring competency, they look for leaders who don't exhibit fear, nor succumb to arrogance.
5. **Stable**—also related to competency; who doesn't want a dependable, mature leader capable of self-control?
6. **Unselfish**—great leaders know when to be generous; they're fair-minded and capable of loyalty.
7. **Cooperative**—great leaders foster a cohesive culture through being broad-minded and collaborative in nature.

8. **Energetic**—without resiliency, determination and ambition, progress can't be sustained.
9. **Accessible**—work commitment is strengthened by having a leader we relate to, and identify with as a caring, real human being.
10. **Positive**—people follow people they like, those who are supportive, upbeat, and show good will.

APPENDIX B:

Top Ten Branding Objectives

1. **Faithful**—a great brand aims to be eternal and, therefore, guards its integrity.
2. **Reflective**—a great brand mirror the deeply held beliefs of its target market because it's always best to sell people on themselves and what they have internalized.
3. **Aspirational**—a great brand enhances its members' self-identities by affirming who they want to be, serving as a bridge to a community to which they long to belong.
4. **Promising**—a great brand is a myth perched atop functional attributes that deliver on the brand promise and make the story feel like reality; because faith adds intensity to the quality of the offer, focus on transcending the rationally-oriented offer.
5. **Exclusive**—a great brand honors people's instinct to belong to an inner circle; without an opposition, a "them," there's no chance for an "us."
6. **Gender-Sensitive**—a great brand may tilt masculine or feminine given the nature of the offer and category; but in defining its personality and associations, a brand should offer something to both genders as appropriate.

7. **Adaptive**—beliefs rarely change much, but in reinforcing them a great brand monitors the ever-changing competitive environment to remain relevant.
8. **Narrative**—a great brand taps into needs and wants so rich and deep that they move the offer from fact to fiction by building an extra protective layer of value around it.
9. **Personable**—create a brand with a personality people can relate to, rather than settling for merely having an awareness-based, generic identity.
10. **Imagistic**—using signature imagery and references, great brands establish an interwoven network of associations that guide people to the brand by influencing what they see and remember.

APPENDIX C:

Top Ten Communications Goals

1. **Hopeful**—address the human desire for something big, new and positive; sell possibilities, and how the offer will emotionally benefit people.
2. **Relevant**—never forget the WIIFM (what's in it for me?); relevancy drives connection; tap into a core motivation, so that a fleeting desire is instead now seen as a necessity.
3. **Visually-Driven**—a combination of *show, don't tell* and *tell a story* works best; anchor the execution with an arresting image, and solve the problem visually.
4. **Believable**—keeping it conceptually simple means giving consumers a single, striking reason to care that fits the core benefit of your offer and is, therefore, plausible.
5. **Values-Driven**—great advertising works because it squares with the target market's beliefs, gaining support by linking to the familiar that's already been emotionally endorsed.
6. **Understandable**—keeping it simple in execution means avoiding *message-itis,* fewer words, a central image to support the

main idea (central truth); let viewers close the loop themselves, subconsciously.

7. **Personalized**—the intimacy that breeds an emotional connection requires that you talk naturally, don't rush, don't shout, and provide close-ups of faces.
8. **Memorable**—great advertising is new but not too new, using unexpected juxtapositions to be both provocative and yet readily understood.
9. **Dynamic**—motion rules, requiring executions that have a flow, a rhythm, a peak; end on a high note to leverage the call to action.
10. **Reassuring**—great advertising enables acceptance by overriding concerns and promoting faith in the offer; it does so in part by providing an intellectual alibi—a reason to believe—but mostly it's a matter of protecting believability by not making any false steps.

APPENDIX D:

Definitions of 10 Emotional States

1. **True Smile**—Strongest of all positive emotional responses, it has the highest possible appeal (50) and impact (50) scores.
   Characterized by: Cheeks rise, and the corners of the mouth lift. The skin below the eyes also bunches, eyelids droop, and crow's feet pinch together.
2. **Robust Smile**—Strong social "false" smile, which shows some appeal and impact but not to the level of a true smile.
   Characterized by: Cheeks rise, teeth show, but there is little if any activity around the eyes.
3. **Weak Smile**—A weaker social smile than the version above.
   Characterized by: There's less rise in the cheeks; the corners of the mouth also lift, but not enough for the teeth to show.
4. **Micro Smile**—A nearly imperceptible social smile, which has the lowest appeal and impact values of all smiles.
   Characterized by: This version of a social smile shows just briefly and on one side of the mouth only.

5. **Surprise—**A neutral emotion that can be either positive or negative depending upon the emotions seen after the surprise has passed.
   Characterized by: Big eyes, raised eyebrows and mouth falling open.
6. **Skepticism—**This is the only emotional state that also incorporates verbal response; it shows disbelief and a lack of enthusiasm.
   Characterized by: A smile while giving a negative response to a question.
7. **Dislike—**A mixture of both disgust and contempt, illustrates when people reject an idea, product, person, etc.
   Characterized by: Nose turns up or wrinkles, upper lip rises, or corner of the mouth twists into a smirk.
8. **Sadness—**Negative reaction showing disappointment or regret.
   Characterized by: Cheeks lift angularly, corners of the eyes crease in a wince.
9. **Frustration—**Annoyance or anger at not being able to make progress, understand something, or otherwise control one's circumstances.
   Characterized by: Eyebrows lower and knit together, eyes narrow (snake eyes), and lips tighten.
10. **Anxiety—**Fear is the most powerful negative emotion because it signals danger.
    Characterized by: Eyebrows lift up and in, eyes widen, lips stretch back horizontally.

APPENDIX E:

How to Read the Charts

EMOTIONAL ENGAGEMENT

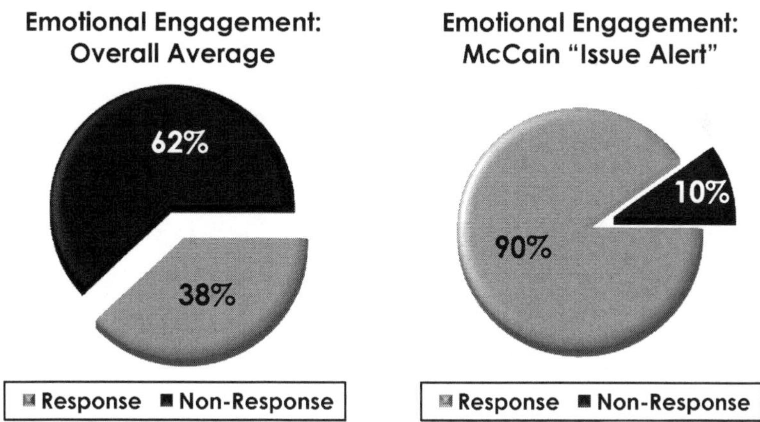

Emotional Engagement: Emotional engagement refers to the percentage of people who had at least one facially-codeable emotional response to the stimulus. As you can see, the McCain attack ad on Romney had a phenomenal level of engagement, which improves the effectiveness of the ad.

APPEAL AND IMPACT, SECOND-BY-SECOND

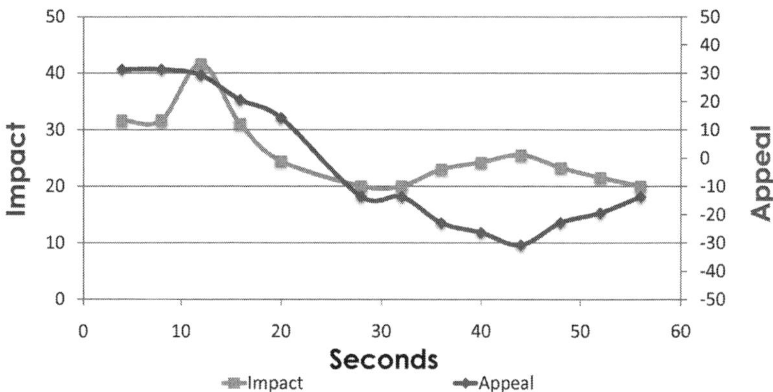

- **Appeal:** Level of positive (or negative) emotion associated with the facially-coded emotional reaction. Scale goes from -50 to 50.
- **Impact:** Level of intensity of the facially-coded emotional reaction. Scale goes from 0 to 50.
- Each second where more than one person had a facially-coded response is indicated with a data point on the second-by-second chart. Each emotional data point indicates the appeal and impact average of all of the people who felt an emotion during that second.

CANDIDATES FACIALLY-CODED DEBATE RESULTS

Candidate	Positive	Neutral	Negative
Democratic Avg.	34%	22%	44%
Dennis Kucinich	69%	8%	23%
Hillary Clinton	62%	23%	15%
John Edwards	50%	21%	29%
Christopher Dodd	38%	0%	63%
Bill Richardson	33%	17%	50%
Barack Obama	30%	30%	40%
Joe Biden	18%	18%	64%
Mike Gravel	9%	45%	45%

- **Positive:** percentage of emotional reactions that were one of the four types of smiles.
- **Neutral:** percentage of emotional reactions that were surprise.
- **Negative:** percentage of emotional reactions that were skepticism, dislike, sadness, frustration or anxiety.

VOTERS REACTIONS TO CANDIDATES

Candidate	Positive	Neutral	Negative
Republican Avg.	9%	6%	85%
Rudy Giuliani	22%	10%	68%
John McCain	13%	3%	84%
Sam Brownback	13%	13%	75%
Fred Thompson	12%	12%	76%
Mitt Romney	9%	6%	84%
Mike Huckabee	0%	8%	92%
Ron Paul	0%	0%	100%
Tom Tancredo	0%	0%	100%

Percentage of voters who were:

- Predominately **Positive** (More than 50% positive emotions)
- **Neutral** (40%—50% positive emotions)
- Predominately **Negative** (Fewer than 40% positive emotions)

APPEAL AND IMPACT, QUADRANT CHART

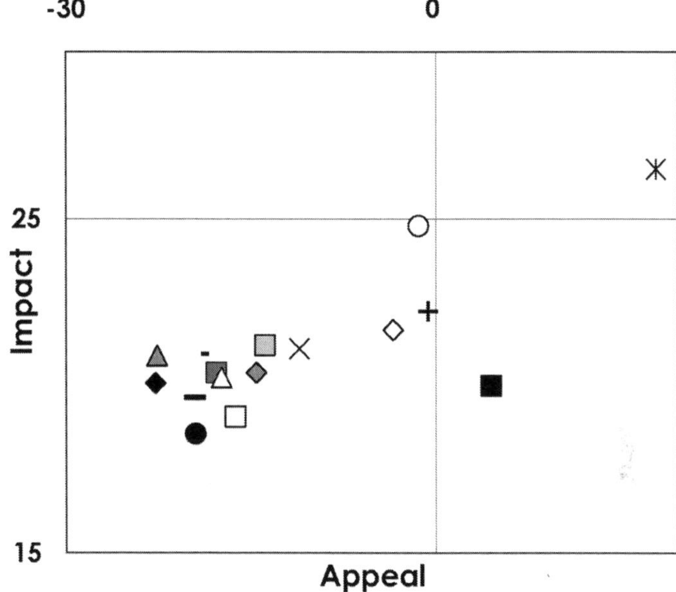

- **Appeal:** Level of positive (or negative) emotion associated with the facially-coded emotional reaction. Scale goes from -50 to 50.
- **Impact:** Level of intensity of the facially-coded emotional reaction. Scale goes from 0 to 50.
- Grid displays the average appeal and impact of all respondents' every emotional reaction to a given stimulus (in this case, campaign commercials). All points are plotted on a grid to compare overall performance.

ENDNOTES

Introduction

1. Mayer, Jeremy D. "Is Death on the Presidential Ballot in 2008?" *Politico* 18 September 2007.
2. Memmott, Mark. "Predictions Burn Pollsters, Pundits – Again." *USA Today* 4 November 2004.
3. Howard, Pierce J. *The Owner's Manual for the Brain.* Atlanta: Bard, 2000.
4. Westen, Drew. *The Political Brain: The Role of Emotion in Deciding the Fate of the Nation*. New York: Public Affairs, 2007.
5. Mahrabian, Albert. *Silent Messages*. Belmont, CA: Wadsworth, 1981.
6. Ekman, Paul. *Emotions Revealed.* New York: Times Books, 2003.
7. Goleman, Daniel. *Emotional Intelligence*. New York: Bantam Books, 1995.
8. Tierney, John. "Political Points: Of Smiles and Sneers." *The New York Times* 18 July 2004.
9. Wolffe, Richard and Daren Briscoe. "Across the Divide: How Barack Obama is shaking up old assumptions about what it means to be black and white in America." *Newsweek* 16 July 2007.
10. McGinniss, Joe. *The Selling of the President*. New York: Penguin Publishing, 1988.
11. Cloud, John. "What's Next 2008: Synthetic Authenticity." *Time* 2007. http://www.time.com/time/specials/2007/0,28757, 1720049,00.html.
12. Gilmore, James. H. and B. Joseph Pine II. *Authenticity: What Consumers Really Want.* Cambridge: Harvard Business School Press, 2007.
13. Canellos, Peter S. "Display Adds to a Storied Lore." *Boston Globe* 10 January 2008.
14. Hill, Dan. *Emotionomics: Winning Hearts & Minds*. Minneapolis: Adams, 2007.
15. Jones, Del. "It's Written All Over Their Faces." *USA Today* 25 February 2008.

Leadership

1. McCain, John and Mark Salter. *Character is Destiny: Inspiring Stories Every Young Person Should Know and Every Adult Should Remember.* New York: Random House Books, 2005.
2. Huckabee, Mike. *Character Makes a Difference: Where I'm From, Where I've Been and What I Believe.* Nashville, TN: B&H Publishing Group, 2007.
3. Huckabee, Mike and John Perry. *"Character Is the Issue: How People with Integrity Can Revolutionize America."* Nashville, TN: B&H Publishing Group, 1997
4. Kouzes, James and Barry Posner. *The Leadership Challenge.* San Francisco: Jossey-Bass, 2002.
5. Powell, Michael and Michael Cooper. "Resurgent McCain is Florida Victor; Guiliani Far Back. Dizzying Fall for Ex-Mayor." *The New York Times* January (2008)
6. Gladwell, Malcolm. *Blink: The Power of Thinking without Thinking.* New York: Little, Brown & Company, 2005.
7. Labrack, Casey. "Candidates' Facial Gestures Grabbing Attention in Race." *American Observer* October (2007); Alarkon, Walter. "Huckabee Would be Smiling VP, Says Psychologist." *Campaigns and Elections* September (2007).
8. Page, Susan. "Support Sags for Giulliani and Clinton in Poll." *USA Today* 4 December 2007.
9. Luo, Michael. "Small Online Contributions Add up to Huge Fundraising Edge for Obama." The New York Times 20 February 2008.
10. Dowd, Maureen. "Savior or Saboteur?" *The New York Times* 23 December 2007.
11. Goleman, Daniel, Richard Boyatzis and Annie McKee. *Primal Leadership: Learning to Lead with Emotional Intelligence.* Boston: Harvard University Press, 2002.
12. Sullivan, Luke. *Hey Whipple, Squeeze This: A Guide to Creating Great Advertising.* New York: Wiley & Sons, 1998.
13. www.YouTube.com
14. Malcolm, Andrew. "Ron Paul's Fund-Raising Fades as Reality Sinks into Followers." Latimes.com *Top of the Ticket* Blog, 21 April 2008.
15. "Paul Abandons Campaign." *St. Paul Pioneer Press* June (2008).
16. Klein, Joe. "Romney's Edge. Nervous Republicans May Prefer a Squeaky-Clean Mormon to a Pro-Choice New Yorker on his Third Marriage." *Time Magazine* 27 August 2007.
17. "Iowa and New Hampshire Voters on the Presidential Race." *The New York Times* 14 November 2007.
18. A collaboration from a number of sources:
    (A) Allik, Jüri, and Anu Realo. "Emotional Experience and Its Relation to the Five-Factor Model in Estonian." *Journal of Personality* 65 (1997): 625-647. EBSCO.
    (B) Chamorro-Premuzic, Tomas, Emily Bennett, and Adrian Furnham. "The Happy Personality: Meditational Role of Trait Emotional Intelligence." *Personality and Individual Differences* 42 (2007): 1633-1639. EBSCO.
    (C) O'Brien, Tess Byrd, and Anita Delongis. "The Interactional Context of Problem -, Emotion-, and Relationship-Focused Coping: the Role of the Big Five Personality Factors." *Journal of Personality* 64 (1996): 775-813. EBSCO.
    (D) Gross, James J., Steven K. Sutton, and Timothy Ketelaar. "Relations

Between Affect and Personality: Support for the Affect-Level and Affective-Reactivity Views." *Personality and Social Psychology Bulletin* 24 (1998): 279-290.
(E) Hudlicka, Eva. "This Time with Feeling: Integrated Model of Trait and State Effects on Cognition and Behavior." *Applied Artificial Intelligence*. Taylor & Francis, 2002. 611-641.
(F) Furnham, Adrian, and K.V. Petrides. "Trait Emotional Intelligence and Happiness." *Social Behavior and Personality* 31 (2003): 815-823. EBSCO.
(G) Deneve, Kristina M., and Harris Cooper. "The Happy Personality: a Meta-Analysis of 137 Personality Traits and Subjective Well-Being." *Psychological Bulletin* 124 (1998): 197-229. EBSCO.
(H) Tong, Eddie M., George D. Bishop, Hwee C. Enkelmann, Yong P. Why, Siew M. Diong, Majeed Khader, and Jansen Ang. "The Role of Big Five in Appraisals." *Personality and Individual Differences* 41 (2006): 513-523. EBSCO.
(I) Watson, David, and Lee Anna Clark. "On Traits and Temperament: General and Specific Factors of Emotional Experience and Their Relation to the Five-Factor Model." *Journal of Personality* 60 (1992): 441-476. EBSCO.
(J) Booth-Butterfield, Steve, and Melanie Booth-Butterfield. "The Role of Affective Orientation in the Five Factor Personality Structure." *Communication Research Reports* 19 (2002): 301-313.

19. Timberg, Robert. *John McCain: An American Odyssey*. New York: Free Press, 2007.
20. Jones, Del. "Besides Being Lonely at the Top, It Can Be 'Disengaging' as Well." *USA Today* 21 June 2005.
21. Dowd, Maureen. "Seeing Red Over Hillary." *The New York Times* 30 January 2008.
22. Andrews, Helena. "Was Hillary Faking" *The Politico* (2008)
23. Dowd, Maureen. "Cry Clinton Cry." *International Herald Tribune*, 9 January 2008.
24. Heilemann, John. "The Fall and Rise of Hillary Clinton." *New York Magazine* 15 June 2008.
25. Heilemann, John. "The Fall and Rise of Hillary Clinton." *New York Magazine* 15 June 2008.

Branding

1. Steele, Shelby. *A Bound Man: Why We Are Excited about Obama and Why He Can't Win*. New York: Free Press, 2008.
2. Marcus, George. "The Structure of Emotional Appraisal: 1984 Candidates." *American Political Science Review* (1988).
3. Powell, Michael and Michael Cooper. "Resurgent McCain is Florida Victor; Guiliani Far Back." *The New York Times* 30 January 2008.
4. Healy, Patrick and Michael Cooper. "Clinton is Victor, Defeating Obama; McCain Also Wins. Tables Are Turned in New Hampshire - New Yorker Expects Costly Fight." *The New York Times*. 9 January 2008.
5. Mooney, Alexander. "$40 Million Spent to Tout Candidates on Iowa TV." *CNN*, 1 January 2008.
6. Knowlton, Brian, Patrick Healy and Michael Cooper. "New Hampshire Primary Provides Comebacks for Clinton and McCain." *International Herald-Tribune* 9 January 2008.
7. Bernstein, Carl. *A Woman in Charge: The Life of Hilary Rodham Clinton*. New York: Vintage, 2007.

8. Schechter, Cliff. *The Real McCain: Why Conservatives Don't Trust Him and Why Independents Shouldn't.* California: PoliPoint, 2008.
9. Mendell, David. *Obama: From Promise to Power.* New York: HarperCollins, 2008.
10. Zeleny, Jeff and Patrick Healy. "Issues Take Back Seat at Debate as Obama and Clinton Tangle." *The New York Times* 2 March 2008.
11. Luo, Michael. "McCain's Victory Muddles G.O.P. Field as It Looks to Michigan." *The New York Times,* 9 January 2008.
12. Will, George. "Of Tulips and Fred Thompson" *Newsweek* 18 June 2007.
13. Broder, David "To Keep the White House, GOP Should Nominate McCain and Huckabee." *The Washington Post* 2 December 2007.
14. Dickinson, Tim. "The Real Liberal: John Edwards Is Third in the Polls, But Don't Count Him Out." *Rolling Stone,* 23 August 2007.
15. Powell, Michael. "Guiliani Tempers Tough Image, Trading the Growl for a Smile." *The New York Times* 29 May 2007
16. Alter, Jonathan. "Wrong Time for an Urban Cowboy?" *Newsweek* 3 December 2007.
17. Haberman, Clyde "Call Him an Oddball If You Must, But Do Call." *The New York Times* 25 September 2007
18. Alter, Jonathan. "Wrong Time for an Urban Cowboy?" *Newsweek* 3 December 2007.
19. Dowd, Maureen. "All About Eve." The New York Times May 2008
20. Barletta, Martha. "Marketing to Women." *Bank Marketing* 1 October 2003.
21. Parker, Kathleen. "Not Just Any Woman." *USA Today* 8 May 2008.
22. Steele, Shelby. *A Bound Man: Why We Are Excited about Obama and Why He Can't Win.* New York: Free Press, 2008.
23. McGirt, Ellen. "The Brand Called Obama." *Fast Company* 24 April 2008.
24. McGirt, Ellen. "The Brand Called Obama." *Fast Company* 24 April 2008.
25. Kristol, William. "The Mask Slips." *The New York Times* 14 April 2008
26. Mendell, David. *Obama: From Promise to Power.* New York: HarperCollins, 2007.

Communications

1. Packer, George. "The Fall of Conservatism." *The New Yorker.* 26 May 2008.
2. Timberg, Robert. John McCain: An American Odyssey. New York: Free Press, 2007.
3. Schecter, Cliff. *The Real McCain: Why Conservatives Don't Trust Him and Why Independents Shouldn't.* Sausalito, CA: PoliPoint, 2008.
4. Schecter, Cliff. *The Real McCain: Why Conservatives Don't Trust Him and Why Independents Shouldn't.* Sausalito, CA: PoliPoint, 2008.
5. Schecter, Cliff. *The Real McCain: Why Conservatives Don't Trust Him and Why Independents Shouldn't.* Sausalito, CA: PoliPoint, 2008.
6. Rubenzer, Steven J. and Thomas R. Faschingbauer. *Personality, Character & Leadership in the White House.* Washington, D.C.: Potomac Books, 2004.
7. Lawrence, Paul R. and Nitin Nohria. *Driven: How Human Nature Shapes Our Choices.* San Francisco: Jossey-Bass, 2002.
8. Seeyle, Katharine and Leslie Wayne. "The Web Takes Ron Paul

for a Ride." *The New York Times*, 11 November 2007.

9. Seelye, Katharine Q. and Leslie Wayne. "The Web finds Ron Paul, and takes him for a ride." *International Herald Tribune*
10. "The GOP Favorite, McCain Lags Online." *The Trail*, washingtonpost.com. 13 February 2008.
11. "The GOP Favorite, McCain Lags Online." *The Trail*, washingtonpost.com. 13 February 2008.
12. Evans, Li. "2008 Presidential Candidates' Online Marketing Strategies." www.searchmarketinggurus.com, 26 December 2007.
13. Evans, Li. "2008 Presidential Candidates' Online Marketing Strategies." www.searchmarketinggurus.com, 26 December 2007.
14. "Hillary '1984'" YouTube. http://www.youtube.com/watch?v=FJklyhWniDQ
15. Albanesius, Chloe. "Study: Voters Increasingly Turning to Web." PCMag.com, June 6, 2008.
16. http://www.youtube.com/
17. Collins, Gail. "Hillary's Free Pass." *The New York Times*, January 10, 2008.
18. Brooks, David. "A Defining Moment." *The New York Times*, March 4, 2008.
19. Stanley, Alessandra. "Firing Barbs, But Looking Like a Saint." *The New York Times*, April 14, 2008.
20. Carter, Joe. "Washington Briefing Straw Poll Results." *Family Research Council Blog* www.frcblog.com.
21. Mooney, Brian. "Stunned by New Hampshire, Pollsters Regroup to Seek Answers." *The Boston Globe*. 10 January 2008.
22. Weiss, Joanna and Amy Farnsworth. "Pundits Among Primary's Biggest Losers." *The Boston Globe*. 10 January 2008.
23. Kronholz, June. "Talk Is Cheap in Politics, But a Deep Voice Helps." *The Wall Street Journal*, November 3, 2007.
24. Will, George F. "Yankee Fan Go Home." *The Washington Post*, 8 May 2008.
25. Seelye, Katherine and John Broder. "2 States May See Delegates Halved." *The New York Times*, 29 May 2008.
26. Wood, Gaby. "How the East Wing is Won." *The Observer*, 4 March 2007.
27. Farhi, Paul. "Cable's Clout." *American Journalism Review*, June/July 2008.
28. Klein, Joe. "Shrinking Democrats." *Time*, May 5, 2008.
29. Powell, Michael and Michael Cooper. "For Giuliani, a Dizzying Free-Fall." *The New York Times*, 30 January 2008.

General Election

1. Mendell, David. *Obama: From Promise to Power.* New York: HarperCollins, 2007.
2. Timberg, Robert. *McCain: An American Odyssey.* New York: Free Press, 2007.
3. Schecter, Cliff. *The Real McCain: Why Conservatives Don't Trust Him and Why Independents Shouldn't.* California: PoliPoint, 2008.
4. Mendell, David. *Obama: From Promise to Power.* New York: HarperCollins, 2007.
5. Mendell, David. *Obama: From Promise to Power.* New York: HarperCollins, 2007.
6. Timberg, Robert. *McCain: An American Odyssey.* New York: Free Press, 2007.

7. Mendell, David. *Obama: From Promise to Power.* New York: HarperCollins, 2007.
8. Mendell, David. *Obama: From Promise to Power.* New York: HarperCollins, 2007.
9. Lawrence, Paul R. and Nitin Nohria. *Driven: How Human Nature Shapes Our Choices.* San Francisco: Jossey-Bass, 2002.
10. Wikipedia. "Heights of United States Presidents and Presidential Candidates."
11. Gladwell, Malcolm. *Blink: The Power of Thinking without Thinking.* New York: Little, Brown & Company, 2005.
12. Packer, George. "The Fall of Conservatism." *The New Yorker.* 26 May 2008.
13. Packer, George. "The Fall of Conservatism." *The New Yorker.* 26 May 2008.
14. Meckler, Laura. "'Generation Gap' Widens in the 2008 Electorate." *The Wall Street Journal,* 2008 July 24.
15. Meckler, Laura. "'Generation Gap' Widens in the 2008 Electorate." *The Wall Street Journal,* 2008 July 24.
16. CBS News/*New York Times* Poll conducted July 7-14. Courtesy of: http://www.pollingreport.com/iraq.htm.
17. Pew Research Center. "Likely Rise in Voter Turnout Bodes Well for Democrats." 10 July 2008.
18. Meckler, Laura. "'Generation Gap' Widens in the 2008 Electorate." *The Wall Street Journal,* 2008 July 24.
19. Collaboration of a number of polls. Courtesy of: http://www.pollingreport.com/BushJob.htm.
20. Shear, Michael D. and Jonathan Weisman. "McCain Undercut by Adviser's Views." *The Washington Post* 11 July 2008.
21. "8 in 10 Americans Say U.S. on Wrong Track" *St. Paul Pioneer Press* 20 June 2008.
22. Mendell, David. *Obama: From Promise to Power.* New York: HarperCollins, 2007.
23. Nagourney, Adam and Megan Thee. "Poll Finds Obama Candidacy Isn't Closing Divide on Race." *The New York Times,* 16 July 2008.
24. Johnson, Glen. "McCain Aide Says Terrorist Attack Would Be Big Help to His Campaign." *St. Paul Pioneer Press,* 23 June 2008.
25. Saad, Lydia. "Presidential Candidates' Weaknesses in Depth." *Gallup,* 2 April 2008.
26. Davis, Susan. "WSJ/NBC Poll: Obama Maintains Lead Over McCain." *The Wall Street Journal,* 23 July 2008.
27. Nagourney, Adam. "A Struggle for Obama: Getting the White Vote." *International Herald Tribune* 24 April 2008.
28. CNN Election Center 2008: Democratic Results. http://www.cnn.com/ELECTION/2008/primaries/results/scorecard/#D.
29. "The Black Population: 2000." Census 2000 Brief. http://www.census.gov/prod/2001pubs/c2kbr01-5.pdf.
30. Nagourney, Adam and Megan Thee. "Poll Finds Obama Candidacy Isn't Closing Divide on Race." *The New York Times,* 16 July 2008.

PHOTO CREDITS

COVER

McCain: Courtesy of: Henry Rome, *The Spoke* (Conestoga High School) 15 April 2008.

Obama: Courtesy of: SEIU International: http://flickr.com/photos/seiu/374553972/.

LEADERSHIP

Pg. 29 Wikimedia Commons, Source: http://www.20minutos.es/imagen/755297

Pg. 31 *Clinton:* Flickr, User: Taekwonweirdo
Rumsfeld & Bush: Flickr, Source: Department of Defense
Cheney: Wikimedia Commons, Source: http://pristina.usmission.gov/images6/chen2.jpg

Pg. 34 *Huckabee:* Flickr, User: candid
Obama: Flickr, User: seiu_international

Pg. 40 Flickr, User: dfred

Pg. 42 Wikimedia Commons, Source: U.S. Congress

Pg. 49 Flickr, User: bmcvey

BRANDING

Pg. 63 *Kennedy:* Wikimedia Commons, Source: Executive Office of the President of the U.S. *Clinton:* Wikimedia Commons, Source: Executive Office of the President of the U.S. *Obama:* Wikimedia Commons, Source: U.S. Congress

Pg. 68 Wikimedia Commons, Source: U.S. Government

Pg. 70 *Gleason:* Flickr, User: kate* *Richardson:* Flickr, User: MikeSchinkel

Pg. 74 *Edwards:* Flickr, User: John Edwards 2008 *Biden:* Flickr, User: IowaPolitics.com
Dodd: Wikimedia Commons, Source: U.S. Government
Kucinich: Flickr, User: Smellyknee
Gravel: Flickr, User: Mike Disharoon

COMMUNICATIONS

Pg. 89 YouTube, Uploaded by 10usc311

Pg. 98 YouTube, Uploaded by JoeBidendotcom

Pg. 102 YouTube, Uploaded by ParkRidge47

Pg. 111 YouTube, Uploaded by johnedwards

Pg. 116 YouTube, Uploaded by Rayquadian

GENERAL ELECTION

Pg. 130 *Pawlenty:* Courtesy of the State of Minnesota
Crist: Wikimedia Commons, Source: the State of Florida

Pg. 131 *Ridge:* Wikimedia Commons, Source: U.S. Department of Homeland Security
Portman: Wikimedia Commons, Source: U.S. Congress
Fiorina: Wikimedia Commons, Source: Agencia Brasil

Pg. 132 *Kaine:* Courtesy of the Commonwealth of Virginia
Clark: Wikimedia Commons, Source: U.S. Army

Pg. 133 *McCaskill:* Wikimedia Commons, Source: U.S. Congress
Bayh: Wikimedia Commons, Source: U.S. Congress
Napolitano: Wikimedia Commons, Source: U.S. Department of Defense

Pg. 142 YouTube, Uploaded by BarackObamadotcom

Pg. 143 YouTube, Uploaded by JohnMcCaindotcom

INDEX

ACKNOWLEDGEMENTS

If politics is emotional, so is writing a book: joy, despair and gratitude for those who help.

First of all I'd like to acknowledge Sensory Logic staff members who have contributed tremendously to the research, analysis, proofreading and editing for this book, including Dominique DuCharme, Todd Kringlie, Rhonda Farran, Nancy Christensen, Joe Bockman and Kate Cook. I am a lucky man, indeed, to employ a richly talented team and sincerely appreciate their creativity, diligence and herculean efforts in making this book possible.

Thanks to Jay Monroe of James Monroe Design for his valuable expertise in formatting the content and designing the layout of the book and to the people at Beaver's Pond Press for bringing it all together.

I truly appreciate my friend, Paul Schuster, of Brandwrite, for his insights and perspectives regarding the content of this book. Without his apt prodding, I might have settled for a lesser outcome.

Finally, I owe my wife, Karen Bernthal, a significant amount of gratitude for her kind, valuable efforts in editing content. Did I mention her patience, too, while I spent many a night and weekend in front of my computer?

Now it's time to take a walk and relax.

Minneapolis, Minnesota

July 30th, 2008